Table of Contents

Introduction

Survival is ingrained in human nature. Every day, people are forced to struggle through work, illness, and tragedy. In today's apocalypse-obsessed society, a zombie takeover has become a distinct possibility. Therefore, people must learn how to survive a zombie apocalypse to prepare for such a catastrophe. Furthermore, the skills and knowledge required to survive a zombie apocalypse - elimination of enemies, use of weapons, finding shelter, etc. - will also be useful in any disaster situation.

In order to learn how to survive a zombie apocalypse, people must either search online for information or read an elaborate novel. The online information is spread out and hardly accurate and the available books spend more time addressing the adventure of the situation than the knowledge needed to survive. The current literature treats a zombie apocalypse comically. This manual will combine the scattered information from internet and literature sources as well as scientific research to form a comprehensive and useful survival guide. The combination of descriptive topic chapters and straightforward steps will allow the reader to be fully informed on the enemy and prepared to start a new life. The manual will use color coding and rating systems to ensure the reader knows the best procedures to handle any given situation. Above all, the primary purpose of the manual is to help the reader survive.

The Zombie Apocalypse Survival Guide will ensure that all necessary information can be found efficiently through several different features including a quick reference guide and frequently asked questions. These features prevent the user from having to search through the entire manual during emergency situations when obtaining quick information is crucial. To assess danger level, the manual will rank zombies and threats on a scale from one to five with one presenting the lowest threat. Then it will detail how to eliminate the threat based on the ranking. The quick reference guide will give condensed instructions on how to best use this manual.

Quick Reference Guide

Since time is extremely important during a zombie apocalypse, you must make sure you are prepared and have a plan when it begins. There are certain basic steps to take to enhance your chances of survival, and they are described in this chapter.

STEP ONE: ANALYZE THE SITUATION

First, you will need to analyze the situation. You could be anywhere when zombies attack, so you must be ready to act quickly when it happens. You will need to grab an immediate weapon, which could be anything—a crowbar, baseball bat, golf club, tennis racket, plumbing pipe, frying pan, or kitchen knife.[1] Hopefully you will have your Zombie Survival Kit already prepared. If you do, grab it. If you don't have one or it is too far away from your current location to procure safely, do your best to acquire the items outlined in Chapter 1: Survival Kit. Then, tune your radio to your local emergency station to listen to broadcasts and stay informed about the danger. Pay attention to what may be causing zombification, and reference Chapter 2: Becoming a Zombie and Chapter 3: Types of Zombies to learn more about the risks ahead.

STEP TWO: GATHER IMMEDIATE SURVIVORS

Securing locations, an essential step in your survival, requires multiple people. Therefore, you must gather survivors that can be a part of your group. These can be family, friends, neighbors, or people around you when the apocalypse begins. Refer to Chapter 5: Forming a Safety Group for instructions on how to form a group. The best people for your group are people that you already know because you can be sure they are psychologically stable and will do more good than harm.

STEP THREE: FIND TRANSPORTATION

In order to complete the next two steps, you will first need transportation. A car is a good start; however, the gas will eventually run out, and if you are not near a gas station when that happens, your vehicle will be rendered useless. While an SUV or truck can hold many supplies, a dirt bike or even a regular bicycle can travel further. The best option would be a large car in which you could store supplies and a bicycle.

STEP FOUR: UPGRADE YOUR WEAPON

You will need to obtain a reliable weapon if you are going to fight off the oncoming zombies. The most obvious and most dangerous place to obtain such a weapon is a gun store.[2] Although a gun store is a great place to be during a zombie apocalypse, it's also sure to attract attention from others.[2] Instead, go to a department store and search for a weapon there. Refer to Chapter 4: Weapons for an idea of weapons to acquire.

STEP FIVE: FIND A SECURE LOCATION

The most important part of finding a secure location is to get out of densely populated areas. Since these areas will have the most people and therefore the most zombies, you should head for the countryside. A wide, flat, unpopulated area like a farm would be perfect because you can see any potential zombie attackers. Refer to Chapter 6: Structures and Raids for how to secure your location once you find it.

STEP SIX: SURVIVE

You will probably not manage to survive a zombie apocalypse without being confronted by a zombie. Therefore, you must know basic defense techniques for protecting yourself against these assailants. One basic step is to never turn your back on the enemy. If you are in a group, you can turn your backs to each other and rotate to ensure no one is caught off guard.[3] Another key to defense is to choose your weapon wisely. If you have no experience with a gun or cannot risk attracting more zombies with the noise of shooting a gun, then choose a machete or a melee weapon. In addition, layered clothes are a great defense against potential zombie bites and a must-have.

1
Survival Kit

A Zombie Survival Kit is a package of essential tools that is prepared before the apocalypse and stored in an easy-access location. When the catastrophe occurs, you will obtain this pre-made kit and begin the arduous task of survival. With these necessary items already at hand, your survival chances will increase significantly.

The most efficient Zombie Survival Kit contains the following items:

- Backpack
- Water bottle and purification tablets
- Non-perishable food
- Dependable hiking boots
- Change of clothing
- Poncho
- First aid kit
- Map and compass
- Knives
- Matches
- Flashlight
- Radios

BACKPACK

The most important part of the Zombie Survival Kit is the backpack. The backpack needs to be large and sturdy so that it can carry all the required equipment in the kit. It should be waterproof as well to preserve its contents. The ideal backpack contains many pockets so that the contents can be organized into categories such as food, shelter, and tools. A picture of a military-grade backpack that fits all the recommendations for the backpack of the survival kit is shown in Figure 1.

Figure 1: Backpack[4]

WATER BOTTLE AND PURIFICATION TABLETS

A water bottle and purification tablets are necessary so that you can stay hydrated and drink clean water. During any apocalypse, clean water becomes scarce. With water purification tablets, water can be taken from any source and turned into drinking water. You can then store this clean water in your water bottle so you can stay hydrated. An example of a water bottle and portable purification tablets is shown in Figure 2.

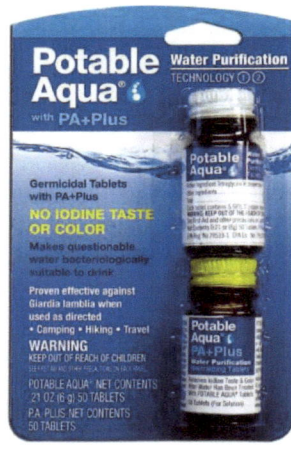

Figure 2: Water Bottle and Purification Tablets[4]

NONPERISHABLE FOOD

Food is also necessary for survival. Since the kit will be in storage before the apocalypse, the packed food must be nonperishable so it doesn't spoil. This is also convenient because no matter how long you go before finding other food, the food in the kit will not spoil. Examples of nonperishable food are ramen noodles, beef jerky, granola, and peanut butter. More examples of nonperishable food are shown in Figure 3.

Figure 3: Nonperishable Food[5]

DEPENDABLE HIKING BOOTS

During a zombie apocalypse, you will be constantly on the move: running from zombies, searching for food and weapons, and securing various locations. All these actions are essential to survival, and all require comfortable, dependable shoes. The best shoes are sturdy hiking boots that will last for years.

CHANGE OF CLOTHING

A change of clothing for the Zombie Survival Kit includes insulated socks, durable pants, a comfortable shirt, and a sturdy jacket. This is important so that if your current garments become wet or damaged, a change of clothing is available. Durable pants and a sturdy jacket are extremely essential, as these will keep zombie bites from breaking one's skin. This will help prevent infection and aid survival.

PONCHO

A poncho is essential survival gear. If your clothes become wet, you can succumb to hypothermia which will severely impair your chances of survival. Therefore, a poncho is necessary to keep you dry. A poncho can also be used to catch rainwater which can be converted to drinking water. Figure 4 depicts a large poncho that would be ideal for this survival kit.

Figure 4: Rain Poncho[4]

FIRST AID KIT

A first aid kit is absolutely necessary to treat wounds and make sure they don't become infected. The first aid kit should contain the following:

- Compress dressings
- Adhesive bandages
- Adhesive cloth tape
- Ointment packets
- Antiseptic wipe packets
- Aspirin
- A breathing barrier
- An instant cold compress
- Non-latex gloves
- Hydrocortisone ointment packets
- Scissors
- Roller bandages
- Gauze pads
- An oral thermometer
- A first aid instruction booklet[4]

This kit can be purchased from the American Red Cross.

MAP AND COMPASS

A map and compass are required for navigation. A map can help when searching for potential living locations or cities for food supplies. A compass is required so that the map can be utilized correctly. The 2013 North America Pocket Road Atlas, shown in Figure 5, can be purchased from Amazon and would be useful for people in North America.[5]

Figure 5: North America Road Atlas[4]

KNIVES

Knives have many uses when surviving a zombie apocalypse including fighting zombies and preparing food. At least two knives are essential for this survival kit. They could also come in handy when building a shelter or breaking into a building for food or shelter.

MATCHES

Fire is necessary for survival in order to cook food and keep you warm. Matches are an efficient way to start a fire, so they are necessary for a survival kit. The best matches are waterproof matches, shown in Figure 7, which stay lit for 15 seconds even after being submerged under water.[5]

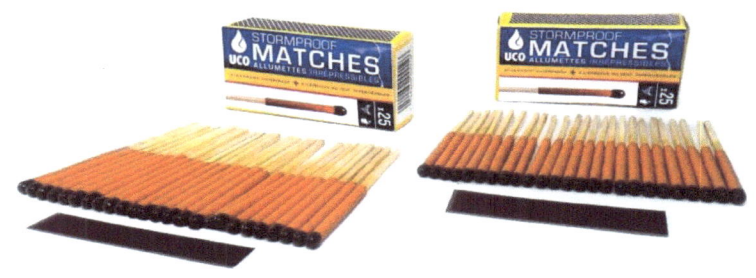

Figure 6: Stormproof Matches[4]

FLASHLIGHT

A flashlight that is solar-powered or crank-operated is essential. This is a great source of light and allows travel at night and through dark locations. It will also help find food in poorly lit basements and stores. If the flashlight is solar-powered or crank-operated, there is no risk of running out of batteries so it can be used for a long time.

RADIOS

Knowledge is key to survival. A radio can broadcast reports of survivors and information about safe locations and extra food, and is therefore essential. A battery-powered radio with lots of extra batteries would be sufficient, but a solar-powered radio would be best. To ensure the radio doesn't become exposed to water and break, a plastic bag should be placed around the radio. Some radios, like the one in Figure 7, are water-resistant and come with Red Cross disaster preparedness tips that can aid survival in any catastrophe.[6] Handheld radios are also important for groups to ensure communication. A pack of walkie-talkies should be packed in the survival kit as well. These can help when your group must split up to secure a building or escape a zombie attack. They will make sure your group can stay in touch.

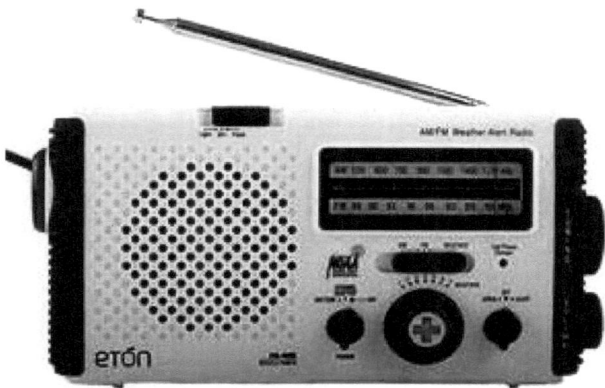

Figure 7: Radio FM/AM/NOAA Bands[6]

A Zombie Survival Kit is a useful set of supplies that will aid survival in any catastrophe, including a zombie apocalypse. In order to be able to use it most effectively, gather the necessary equipment together now and store it in a safe, accessible location. When disaster strikes, this kit will help aid your survival and can be the difference between life and death.

2
Becoming a Zombie

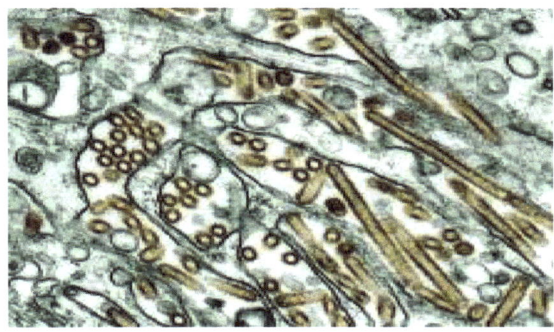

There are several ways that a human can become a zombie, and it is crucial to know the origin of the zombie before facing it. The mention of the undead dates back thousands of years to the *Epic of Gilgamesh*, which details the dead rising from the grave to eat the living.[7] The concept of the dead coming back to life to seek revenge was an important theme throughout ancient mythology and cultural legends. However, when modern science began replacing superstition, the idea of zombies became solely fantasy except in Haitian Vodou (Voodoo). Zombies made an appearance in pop culture in the 1970's because of George Romero's movie series of the undead. Since then, zombie culture has evolved and become more popular, prompting the discussion of a possible undead takeover. Scientists and researchers have theorized that a zombie apocalypse would be possible under certain conditions and under the assumption that a zombie does not have to be a creature that has risen from the dead. There are several ways for a human to become a zombie, but only a few would result in an epidemic or takeover. This chapter will explore the different methods in which humans could become zombies relevant to a zombie apocalypse.

The following are methods of zombification mentioned in this chapter:

- Virus
- Parasite
- Neurotoxin
- Neurogenesis
- Nanobots

VIRUS

A virus is a non-living organism made up of three parts: nucleic acid, a protein coat, and a lipid membrane. The nucleic acid contains the DNA and RNA of the virus. The protein coat protects the DNA/RNA core and the lipid membrane (sometimes not present) covers the protein coat.[8]

How Viruses Function

Viruses cannot survive alone because they are not living organisms. Therefore, they must invade a living host so they can replicate. Viruses must attach to receptors that are specific to the type of host cell they infect. The receptors are located on the surface of the host cell. Viruses from the environment or another host enter a new host through orifices such as airways and wounds. From there, the virus finds a cell to infect and injects its DNA/RNA into the host cell. The DNA/RNA from the virus gains control of the cell's enzymes, which begin replicating the particles that make up the virus. These particles combine to form new virions (virus particles) that kill the cell so that they can invade new cells in the host and continue replicating.[8]

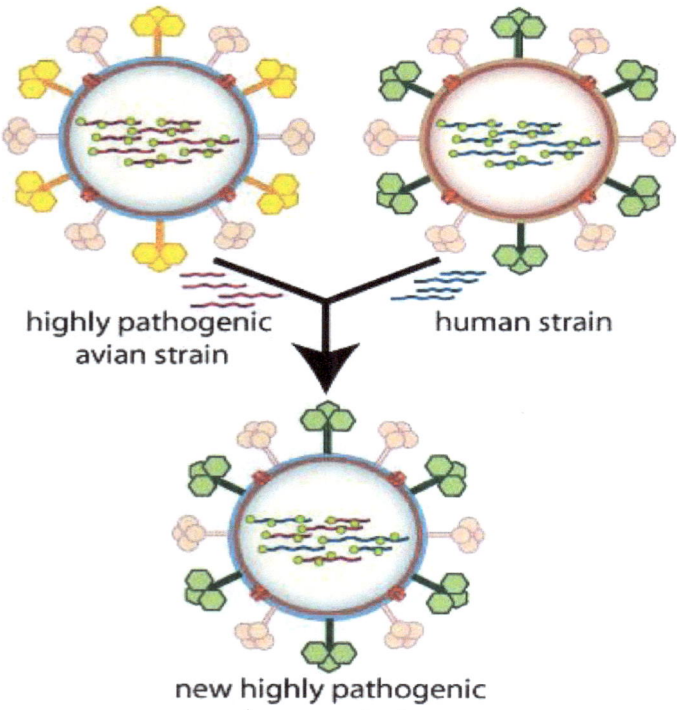

Figure 8: Recombination of Virus DNA[9]

The Evolution of a Zombie Virus

Viruses are highly aggressive organisms and certain strains can cause violent and zombie-like behavior in the host organism. One such strain is the rabies virus, which can cause the host to become hostile and mentally insane. Symptoms of the rabies virus can take anywhere from ten days to one year to manifest, but it would be possible for the incubation period to decrease through genetic mutation or manipulation of the virus. According to virologist Samita Andreansky, if the rabies virus mutated quickly enough, it could cause infection within an hour.[10] However, the virus would also have to become more infectious and be transmittable through the air. It is theoretically possible to mix several viruses that would produce zombie characteristics through modern genetic engineering, but it would be difficult. An example of virus DNA/RNA recombination (mixing the genetic information) is shown in Figure 8.

Threat

(Level 3)

Although it is unlikely that a zombie virus would be successfully engineered in this decade, the science and techniques that could produce such a virus in the future already exist. If a zombie virus becomes a reality, an airborne strain is likely to be more contagious than influenza and more aggressive than ebola. The only way to combat the spread of the virus will be to wear gas masks and to have no contact with infected humans or surfaces. Humans that become zombies in this way will be dangerous because the virus is highly contagious and the behavior of the zombie will be viciously hostile.

PARASITE

A parasite can be a living or non-living organism that lives off of a host organism. There are three main types of parasites that infect humans: protozoa, helminths, and ectoparasites. Protozoa are one-celled and usually transmitted through contaminated food or water or through a vector such as a mosquito. Protozoa cause infectious diseases in humans and multiply inside the host body. Helminths are multicellular organisms, such as tapeworms, but they do not usually cause diseases. Ectoparasites are organisms that require a blood meal from the host and can cause diseases, but more often they carry pathogens and infect the host.[11]

How Parasites Function

Parasites have one goal: survival. They accomplish this goal by feeding from the host and reproducing. Parasites release neuromodulators (substances the nervous system uses to communicate[12]) that modify the host's behavior to benefit the parasite's survival. Furthermore, parasites can affect gene expression and essentially change the host's life cycle.[13] They do not target specific behavioral traits but rather the whole personality of the host. Parasites may direct a host to commit suicide so that the parasite's offspring are released or so that a new host can be infected. One example is a parasite that infects sheep by using ants as an intermediate host. The parasite releases its eggs in a compound that is eaten by snails and the hatched eggs are released by the snail as slime that is then ingested by ants. The ant's behavior is then modified so that it is motivated to climb to the top of a blade of grass and wait until it is eaten by sheep.[14] This process is shown in Figure 9 below. Such strong behavioral alterations are rarely seen in humans, but they are common in animals. There are parasites that cause changes in human behavior and scientists have linked Toxoplasma (a parasite contracted by humans from cats) and schizophrenia.[14]

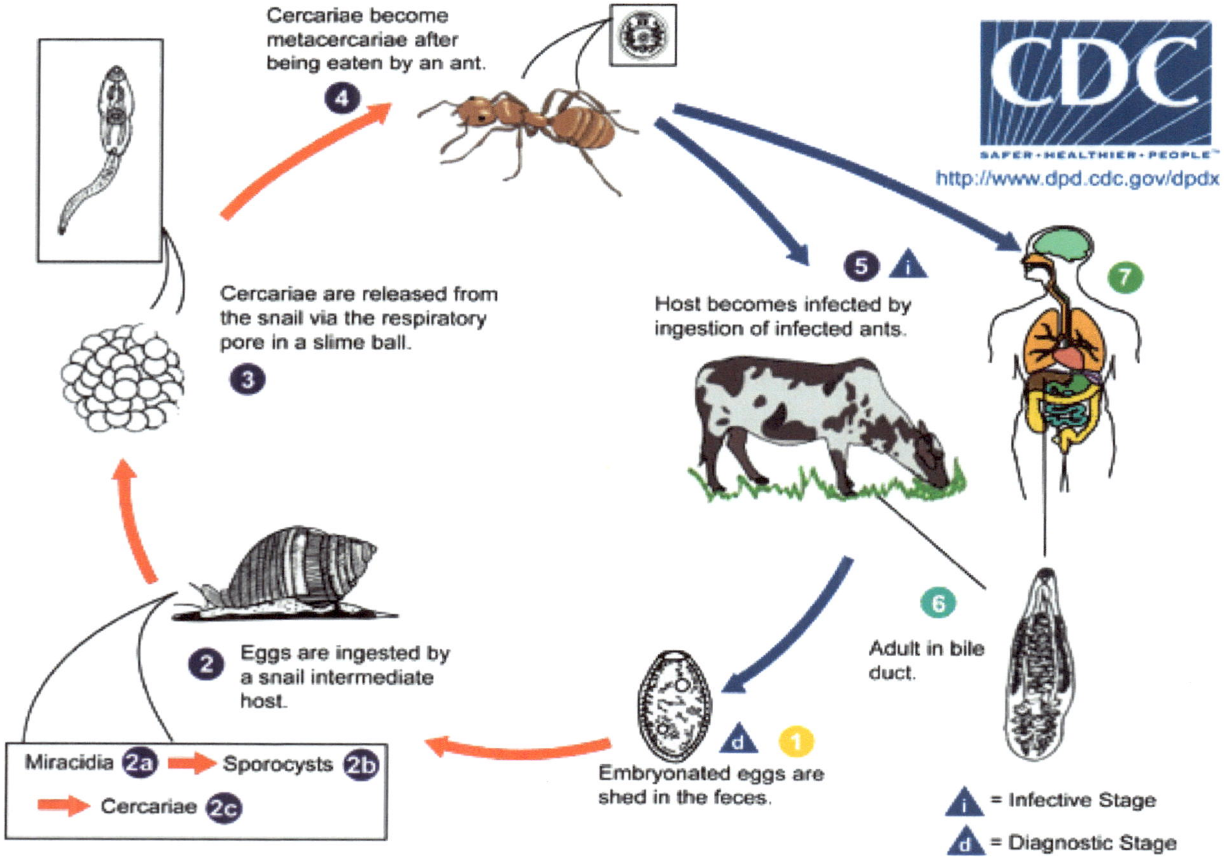

Cercariae become metacercariae after being eaten by an ant.

4

CDC
SAFER·HEALTHIER·PEOPLE™
http://www.dpd.cdc.gov/dpdx

7

5 **i**

Host becomes infected by ingestion of infected ants.

Cercariae are released from the snail via the respiratory pore in a slime ball.

3

6

Adult in bile duct.

2

Eggs are ingested by a snail intermediate host.

Miracidia **2a** → Sporocysts **2b**

→ Cercariae **2c**

d **1**

Embryonated eggs are shed in the feces.

i = Infective Stage

d = Diagnostic Stage

Figure 9: Life Cycle of Dicrocoelium Dendriticum[15]

The Evolution of a Zombie Parasite

Parasites that cause behavioral and functional changes in humans are a reality. One parasite that infects humans, Toxocara canis, causes vision damage and memory loss. Infected humans have also experienced sickness behavior, lethargy, and indifference to danger. Scientists have proven that parasites can initiate changes in the immune system, the nervous system, and the brain to modify behavior so that it mimics basic animal survival.[13] A zombie parasite would transform a human in the same way that all parasites function; it would take control of the host's body systems. The main goal of the parasite would be to infect other humans or use humans as an incubator for the virus. The parasite would manipulate the behavior of the human so that it would be compelled to attack other humans and allow the parasite to enter the bloodstream.

Threat
(Level 4)
Zombie parasites already exist in nature, but their method of infection is on a small scale. At the current rate that aggressive parasites infect humans, a zombie apocalypse would not occur. If an aggressive parasite such as Toxocara canis or Toxoplasma were to use the water or food supply of humans as its method of infection, it would lead to an epidemic of infected humans that exhibit zombie-like behavior. Infected humans would experience an overwhelming desire for survival and to infect other humans using any means. They would lose normal inhibitions and be mentally unstable. Essentially, humans would lose control of their body and minds to the parasite.

OTHER METHODS OF ZOMBIFICATION

There are several methods in which a human can become a zombie, but these methods would not lead to transformation on a global scale. Neurotoxin, neurogenesis, and nanobots are additional ways that a human can develop zombie-like behavior sans the desire for human flesh. Neurotoxins poison the body so that it enters a state similar to death, and after recovery the victim can only perform simple tasks like eating and sleeping. Neurogenesis is the process of using stem cells to regrow organs. Scientists could use neurogenesis to regenerate dead brain cells and reanimate a corpse. Nanobots are small robotic like creatures that could be used to reanimate a corpse by reconnecting neurons in the body. There would only be basic brain functions in a corpse controlled by nanobots. Although these methods can turn a human into a zombie or reanimate a corpse, they are individual transformations; they could not produce a zombie apocalypse.

3
Types of Zombies

When facing any threat, it is vital to fully understand the threat to effectively disarm or destroy it. There are several types of zombies that a survivor might face. Although the description will include all known varieties, rogue zombies that are a combination of the known types could also pose a threat. The following classes of the undead will be described:

- Crawler
- Wanderer
- Runner
- Intellectual (Leader)
- Soldier

The descriptions will include how to identify the zombie types by physical appearance and behavior, the danger presented, and how to eliminate the danger. Until properly trained, it is important not to approach a zombie of any type with an offensive attack. All types of the undead can be dangerous and should only be engaged as a defensive maneuver.

CRAWLER

The crawler is one of the most common types of zombies and though it may seem harmless, it is still a carnivorous predator. Typically, crawlers are among the most decayed and damaged of the undead classes and as such can only move by crawling.

Appearance

At first glance, crawlers may appear fully dead due to the damage they have suffered. They can be identified by decaying flesh, lacerations, odd patchy-colored skin, one or more missing limbs—usually a lower extremity—and the inability to walk. The crawler may have a combination or all of these identifying features, but it will certainly be unable to stand or walk and will have decaying flesh. An example of a crawler is provided below in Figure 16. The degraded flesh, wounds, and inability to walk should be noted in this particular crawler.

![Crawler](Figure 16)

Figure 16: Crawler[16]

Behavior

Normal behavior for crawlers is unintentional solitude. They travel alone with no specific destination and are forever on the hunt for human flesh. Some crawlers may be seen with others, but they will not stay together for long as their ultimate goal is food and once they have separated, it would be difficult and time consuming for them to reunite. In addition, they have no desire for companionship and thus have no reason to travel in groups. If a food source (human) has been identified, several crawlers may focus on that source, which appears to be a group effort, but it is not. They attack already fallen victims or grab at the feet of fleeing humans.

Threat
(Level 1)

Of all the zombie types, crawlers present the lowest threat because of their inability to walk. However, the threat level increases when a survivor is injured or unable to flee. They are more dangerous in groups, especially when the prey is trapped.

Elimination

Crawlers can be eliminated in the same way that all other zombie types can be eliminated: severing the head from the body. The best way to sever the head is to use some form of blade, preferably one with a long range, so that the survivor may keep a distance from the zombie. A short blade should only be used as a last resort because it is neither strong nor sharp enough to quickly sever the head. A shotgun may also be used to separate the head from the body. Most shotgun shells to the head will cause it to explode. There are only two types of zombies upon which basic flame (excluding explosive devices which can be used on all zombies) can be used as an elimination method: the crawler and the wanderer. Setting a crawler or wanderer on fire is effective because it is too slow to attack before the flames engulf its entire body. An explosive device will also be effective at destroying the zombie.

WANDERER

The wanderer is similar to the crawler in that it is a low-level zombie that moves slowly. Although they usually shuffle slowly, some may potentially walk as fast as a human. Be aware of large, seemingly organized groups. They may be controlled by an intellectual or soldier zombie.

Appearance

This zombie may be missing one or more appendages above its torso so that it may still walk. It will usually hold its arms (if any) at awkward angles for balance and its legs may struggle to move normally. Its skin will be decaying, rotten, or gray in color, like that of a corpse. Eyes may be yellowed or bloodshot, but will always appear to be unseeing. A picture of a group of wanderers is provided in Figure 17.

Figure 17: Group of Wanderers[17]

Behavior

Despite its name, the wanderer tends to move in packs with other wanderers, but may also travel alone. If they are moving in small groups, they are not being led by an intellectual or soldier zombie. They can smell the scent of human flesh and though they seem slow, they will not stop hunting once they focus on a scent. They are also scavengers and will eat the flesh of a recently attacked human.

Threat
(Level 2)

The wanderer presents the second lowest threat level because of its lack of intelligence and slow speed. The threat is greater when the wanderers travel in small groups. If there is a large group, they may be led by soldier or intellectual zombies and are highly dangerous. It is similar to a zombie army with attack plans and offensive maneuvers.

Elimination

Severing the head is the best method of elimination. In the case of a wanderer, a survivor should not attempt to use a short range blade. If a small blade is used, a wanderer will most likely bite or kill the survivor in the process. A machete, sword, or other long sharp piece of metal will be the best weapon.

A shotgun can be used to shoot the head of this zombie. A well-aimed explosive device will also eliminate a wanderer or group of wanderers. As with crawlers, setting a wanderer on fire can be effective, but should only be used as a last resort. A survivor should never attempt to set a group of wanderers ablaze because they will become a walking wall of flaming zombies. An example of the result of setting wanderers on fire is shown in Figure 18.

Figure 18: Flaming Zombies[18]

RUNNER

A runner is one type of undead that presents a threat greater than the basic crawlers and wanderers. A runner should never be approached.

Appearance

This type of undead creature may or may not look like a human depending on how it became a zombie. It will not be missing any limbs and most likely will not have wounds, lacerations, or decaying flesh. Its skin will be gray or yellow in color. An example of runners is seen below in Figure 19.

Behavior

Runners may travel alone or in groups. Sometimes the groups are organized by an intellectual and are extremely dangerous. These organized groups are significantly more dangerous than organized groups of wanderers. They cannot think for themselves and present less of a threat alone than in a group.

Figure 19: Runners in a Pack[19]

Threat

A runner is third lowest threat level and in groups, presents the same threat as an intellectual because they are both dangerous, but for different reasons. Runners are extremely quick and may run in short bursts of speed or for long distances. They can easily overtake a human and are able to keep up with cars for short distances. They do not possess intelligence, but instead only a voracious appetite. A human cannot outrun this type of zombie without a vehicle. The only options are to hide in a safe barricade or eliminate the runner.

Elimination

The runner can be eliminated most easily with any type of gun to slow it down and a shotgun to remove the head. Only a survivor experienced with a blade should attempt to sever the head in this way. An explosive device must be aimed and will be ineffective due to the runner's speed. The worst possible method of elimination is attempting to set a runner on fire. A flaming runner is equivalent to a fireball and greatly increases the threat of a runner.

INTELLECTUAL (LEADER)

An intellectual zombie can also be known as a leader zombie because it seeks out groups of other undead classes to use for its own purposes. It will arrange armies to find food and prevent itself from being eliminated by humans.

Appearance

An intellectual may look similar to a wanderer or a runner. It may not be missing any limbs and will not be missing any lower appendages. Unlike wanderers, they have seeing eyes. They are not as swift as runners, but they possess the ability to both walk and run. Figure 14 shows an example of an intellectual zombie using a gun.

Behavior

Intellectuals are solitary in that there will never be two or more intellectuals together. They are highly intelligent and will organize armies of wanderers, runners, or soldiers to seek out food

Figure 14: Intellectual Zombie[20]

sources of human flesh. They will use humans' weapons against them. Intellectual zombies are ruthless and will sacrifice as many other zombies as is necessary to keep themselves from being eliminated.

Threat
(Level 4)

Intellectuals are the second highest threat level of all the zombie types because of their extreme intelligence and high level of functionality. This type of zombie has the ability to do the same tasks as a human including driving a vehicle, using a weapon, and planning organized attacks. Because this zombie is powerful and intelligent, it can bring several of one zombie class or multiple types of zombies together to form one unit. It will then use offensive strategies to take down humans, either for food or to reduce the threat of being eliminated by survivors. Whether alone or leading an army, a survivor should use extreme caution if approached by an intellectual.

Elimination

A human should not try to outsmart an intellectual because it will be one step ahead at all times. The best methods of elimination are using a gun to impede the progress of the zombie and then an explosive device, such as a grenade to destroy the entire body, or a long blade to sever the head. A shotgun might also be effective to remove the head of the intellectual. Fire is not effective because of the zombie's intelligence and speed. It will also be able to use a weapon against the survivor even if it is ablaze.

SOLDIER

Soldier zombies were formerly part of some trained military, whether it was the army, navy, or marines. They are highly trained in combat and weaponry and are extremely dangerous.

Appearance

A soldier zombie may look like a wanderer with decaying flesh, wounds, and the possibility of missing limbs. The skin will be gray, yellow, or appear bruised and may be rotting. It will be wearing some form of military clothing and may possess weapons. A soldier zombie is shown in Figure 15.

Behavior

Soldier zombies usually travel in troops as they did when they were human soldiers. They execute attacks that they would have used when they were living. Though they do not possess great intelligence, they are highly trained fighters and have knowledge of battle and combat strategy. Soldier zombies are extremely strong, but they are always looking for the leadership of an intellectual. They will attack strongholds of survivors, but will not hesitate to make any lone survivor their next victim.

Threat
(Level 5)

This type of zombie presents the greatest threat level because most survivors that go up against a platoon of soldier zombies will be killed. They are skilled in combat and weaponry and they are extremely strong. Only a human soldier or highly trained survivor will be able to engage a soldier zombie.

Figure 15: Soldier Zombie[21]

Elimination

The best method of elimination is to use an explosive device to destroy an entire platoon of soldier zombies or a shotgun aimed at the head to destroy a single zombie. It is not effective to use fire against this zombie because it can still use weapons and hand-to-hand combat to take down a survivor. It may be possible to outrun a soldier zombie as they are not very quick. However, hiding is not the best option because they tend to travel in groups.

4
Weapons

In the face of a threat, the proper weapon can be a survivor's best friend. There are three different types of weapons that you are most likely to come across during a zombie apocalypse. They are:

- Gun
- Blade
- Flame device

Detailed descriptions of each of these weapon categories is to follow, along with information on how to locate (or create) the weapons, and how to use them. It is important to understand that all weapons should be used only as a last resort for defense, and not in an aggressive, attacking manner.

GUN

Perhaps the most powerful personal protection device is the gun, defined as "a device which throws a projectile."[22] Guns are very diverse in type and form, and so only a general description will be given here. They all generally consist of a handle or grip, a barrel, and a trigger mechanism. The handle is for holding the gun, while the barrel is where the projectile exits the weapon. The trigger mechanism, when pulled, causes the gun's internal mechanisms to fire and shoot a projectile. All weapons, especially guns, can be injurious to the user if used incorrectly, so individuals should only use one if properly trained and familiar with them.

Handgun

Handguns can be useful personal protection devices because they can be easily concealed and are easily carried. Handguns are typically less than a foot in length and are light enough to be held with one hand, although it is preferable to use two hands during operation. The handgun may be used as a deterrent weapon for runners **(Level 3)** and intellectuals **(Level 4)** or as an elimination weapon for crawlers **(Level 1)** or wanderers **(Level 2)**. A picture of a semi-automatic pistol, one type of handgun, is provided in Figure 20 below.

Figure 20: Handgun[23]

Rifle

Rifles are longer-barreled than a handgun, and always require two hands to operate. They fire only one bullet at a time with greater accuracy. They are usually used to strike an enemy from a distance, but they can be used in closer quarters. A rifle cannot be used as an elimination weapon because it fires small single bullets instead of exploding shells. It is an effective deterrent weapon against the runner **(Level 3)** and intellectual **(Level 4)**. Rifles can be more difficult to carry due to their larger size, which can be seen in Figure 21.

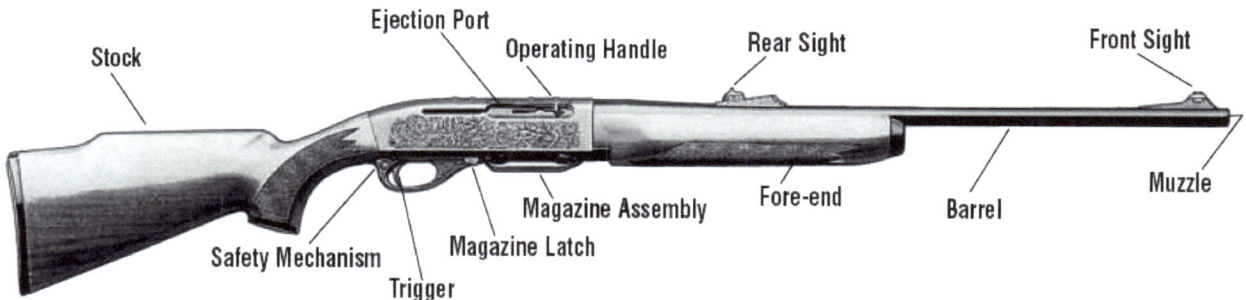

Figure 21: Remington Rifle[23]

Shotgun

The last common type of gun is a shotgun. Shotguns are similar in shape and size to a rifle. In fact, some shotguns today actually have a spiral in their barrel, something that used to differentiate rifles from them.[23] However, the biggest difference is in the purpose. Shotguns are used at very close range, and instead of a bullet they oftentimes have essentially exploding pellets. This makes shotguns easy to use, in that they must only be pointed, not aimed. They can be ideal in situations where a quick reaction may be necessary, and steady aim is difficult to come by. A shotgun works effectively against all types of zombies **(Levels 1-5)** and is the best type of weapon to eliminate them. However, some shotguns can only fire two shots at a time, and ammunition is difficult to find. A photo of a shotgun is provided in Figure 22 below.

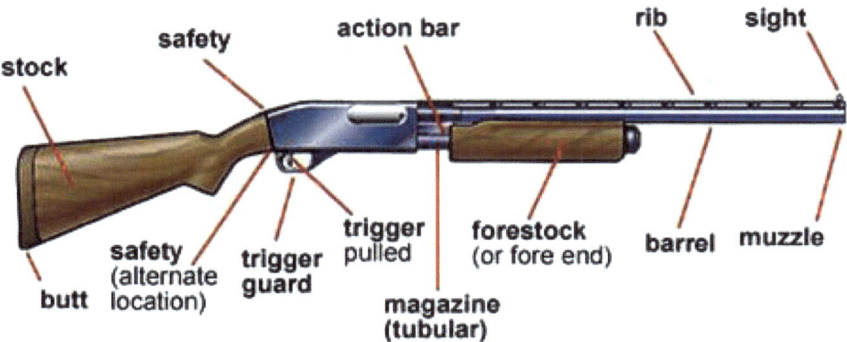

Figure 22: Shotgun[23]

Where to Find a Gun

Many households and sporting goods stores have guns. In an emergency situation, such as a zombie apocalypse, these are the best places to start looking. Since they are inherently dangerous, they are often kept locked up safely; this can make finding them more difficult.

Operating a Gun

The most important thing about operating a gun is that the operator must treat it with respect. It is enormously powerful, and it can be dangerous in the wrong hands. Only trained, experienced users should operate such a weapon, and they should follow all safety precautions that are described in standard training.

The first step of operating a gun is releasing the safety device. The safety keeps the gun from firing accidentally. Next, the operator should hold the gun with proper form. This usually means an upright, comfortable position. Rifles and shotguns are usually held near the shoulder, while handguns are held with either one or two hands extended outward from the body. The user should then locate their target and line the barrel of the gun up with the target. Some guns have scopes, which use crosses and lasers to making aiming easier. Lastly, the operator moves his or her finger to the trigger mechanism and pulls it. The projectile will then fire.

BLADE

Blade-type weapons, like guns, are also quite familiar to most people. Blade weapons can be anything that has a sharp edge. Most blades are made of metal, such as swords, machetes, and knives. They also usually have a handle which allows for comfortable handling and protects the user from coming in contact with the blade and injuring themself. Blades are designed for close encounters but relatively useless from afar.

Figure 23: Pocket Knife[24]

Locating a Blade

Anything with a sharp edge can be used as a blade, provided it can be easily and safely handled. Pocket knives are common items which can be found relatively easily; a photo of one is provided in Figure 23. Other types of blades can be more difficult to find, so it may be necessary to search extensively for them.

Operating a Blade

Zombies are usually afraid of blades by nature. While guns may be difficult for their decaying brain to analyze, a blade's purpose is quite clear. This fear can be useful, as the best weapon is the one which never has to be used. The first way to use a blade is in a slashing motion. A slashing motion requires the user to move the blade quickly from one direction to another. Swinging the blade at the target in this way can seriously injure a zombie. Another way to use a blade is in a jabbing motion. Jabbing with a blade is similar to poking someone in the arm with a finger. The blade is extended and pushed towards the target. Blades are useful weapons in a defense situation, but they should be used with care. A long range blade, such as a machete, is most useful in eliminating crawlers **(Level 1)**, wanderers **(Level 2)**, and intellectuals **(Level 4)** by severing the head. A survivor should not attempt to engage a runner **(Level 3)** or soldier **(Level 5)** zombie with a blade unless highly trained.

FLAME DEVICE

A flame is defined as any type of fire, but in a defensive context, it usually requires that the flame is able to be easily wielded. Torches involve a flame perched on top of a handle, which allows for easy maneuverability. Another useful type of flame device is a flamethrower, which can be thought of as a gun which shoots out a stream of fire. Lastly, Molotov cocktails and other types of homemade incendiary devices can be useful. Such a device is similar to a small grenade that can cause a fire.

Locating a Flame Device

Most flame devices are not found so much as they are made. Some of the necessary materials for making them include wood/brush, gasoline, and rags. Wood and brush can be found easily along the edges of forests and wooded areas. Gasoline is a precious commodity during a zombie apocalypse, and it can be difficult to find. The best places to find it, however, are the most obvious: gas stations, tankers, vehicles, and, in smaller quantities, households.

Creating a Molotov Cocktail

Molotov cocktails are simple to make. First, moisture is completely removed from an empty, breakable bottle. Then, a flammable liquid (likely gasoline or alcohol) is poured into the bottle up to the neck. If possible, it is best to stuff the bottle's neck with a cork to make it easier to throw. A rag tied around the body of the bottle is lit on fire, and then the Molotov is tossed towards the target. On impact, the bottle breaks, allowing the lit rag to ignite the fuel inside.

Operating a Flame Device

Depending on the type of zombie apocalypse occurring, a flame can be the greatest weapon of all for self-defense. Some zombies are inherently nocturnal, choosing to stick to the shadows and darkness of night. By nature, zombies are afraid of what they are not used to, and so they often fear light. Simply carrying a torch or keeping a camp fire can be useful as a "weapon" of sorts. Torches can be used to light things on fire or they can be used in much the same way blades are used. Molotov Cocktails can be thrown at the zombie or near another area that needs burned but cannot be easily reached. Flame devices such as a torch or flamethrower can be used in the elimination of the crawler **(Level 1)** or wanderer **(Level 2)** zombie as described in Chapter 3: Types of Zombies. A flame device such as a grenade or Molotov cocktail will effectively eliminate intellectual **(Level 4)** and soldier zombies **(Level 5)**.

CONCLUSION

Almost anything can be used as a weapon if the person using it is creative enough. Guns are the most powerful weapon, and can be used in many situations and from a variety of distances. They are also the most dangerous to the operator, as improper use can result in injury or even death. Blades are mostly used in close, hand-to-hand encounters with zombies. They do not provide much of a threat from a distance, unless they are thrown like a dagger. Lastly, flame devices provide the user with a unique advantage over zombies: fear. Although hard to control, flame devices can certainly serve a purpose during a zombie apocalypse. There are other types of weapons, but these three categories are the most readily available during a disaster situation. Use each with caution, and avoid conflict whenever possible.

5

Forming a Safety Group

Just as wolves travel in a pack to ensure survival, apocalypse survivors should find a trustworthy group of individuals for security. The following set of instructions will provide you with the information you need to locate survivors and establish a safety group. This is one of the most important steps of surviving a zombie apocalypse. Be sure to read and understand all of the instructions listed before beginning them.

PREREQUISITES

These instructions assume that you:

- have safely escaped any immediate danger.
- have found a reliable source of food and water.
- are alone or with a small group and could benefit from interacting with others.

HOW TO FORM A SAFETY GROUP

1) Attempt to contact neighbors, friends, and family using pre-apocalyptic communication techniques. This can include calling them, emailing them, or travelling to their house.

 Note: It is unlikely that all of these techniques will be feasible. Use your best judgment to avoid putting yourself or others in harm's way.

2) Search through radio frequencies using a standard AM/FM radio to see if other survivors may be attempting to contact others and form a group.

3) Carefully search for people in areas that are likely to still be populated. Highways, town centers, and grocery stores are places people will naturally gravitate towards in times of emergency.

4) Before approaching anyone, be sure that they are not zombies. Use the Chapter 3: Types of Zombies to become familiar with and to learn to identify zombies. Figure 24 below is one example of what a zombie may look like.

Figure 24: A Typical Zombie[25]

 Warning: If you have any doubts as to whether someone is a zombie or a rogue dangerous survivor, do not approach them! The risk far outweighs the reward.

5) Make it clear to the person that you are not a zombie. Hold your hands up above your head to show you mean no harm. Clearly state your name to them. If you know the person, state something the two of you have done or seen together. Demonstrate your

still-human level of intelligence by listing state capitals, saying the alphabet, or naming previous presidents.

6) Tell the other person to complete similar actions as those listed in step 5 to ensure that they are also uninfected.

 Note: Leader zombies can be surprisingly normal in appearance. However, their communication skills will be extremely limited when not speaking to other zombies.

7) Explain to the other person that you wish to establish a group for mutual protection. Convince them that they should join the group. The following points can be useful:

- Sharing resources can benefit the whole group by allowing for specialization.
- Everyone can share what they have learned about the zombies and the particular form of outbreak so that you may better prepare yourself for the danger ahead.
- It is easier to fend off zombies when in groups.
- It may eventually be possible to build a fortified colonization free from infection.
- Some uninfected humans will form rogue groups. They can be extremely dangerous, and are most easily dealt with as a group.
- Securing locations is best done in a group.

The situation may dictate that some of these arguments are moot points. In addition, you may be able to come up with some of your own more appropriate arguments for forming a group.

8) Once you have formed a group of at least 10 willing adults, you must establish a way of organizing those members. Since desperate times require quick decision-making, ensure that a good deal of power rests in the hands of a capable few. Democratic decision-making should be left for less-pressing decisions, such as whether it is prudent to begin travelling to the countryside. At the very least, your group will require a single executive leader and 3-5 advisers with useful knowledge, such as a farmer.

9) Collectively come up with an intelligent way of identifying yourself to the rest of the group. Use complex handshakes, gestures, or phrases to make identifying one another easy and safe.

Caution: Always assume someone is infected unless you are absolutely sure they are not. Require those around you to identify themselves uniquely in a way that a zombie would not be able to replicate.

6
Structures and Raids

Structures are important places during the zombie apocalypse for supplies and shelter. Survivors will have to find buildings for various reasons, but during the outbreak structures will be infested with zombies and it's important to know what buildings to raid. Raiding is clearing out a building for the sake of resupplying, which is dangerous and should only be done as a group. The common buildings analyzed in this chapter are:

- Hospital
- Supermarket
- Apartment Complex
- Suburban House
- Convenience Store
- Police Station
- Farm

The factors that will be analyzed are a description of the building, the risks of the building during the apocalypse, the rewards for raiding the building, a general description of how to raid the building, and whether or not the building is a possible short term or long term shelter.

HOSPITAL

Hospitals are places that treat the ill and perform surgical operations on the injured. To accommodate a large amount of patients, hospitals are generally big and centrally located in most cities. All towns have some form of a hospital or a healing center that provides treatment, medicine, and recovery.

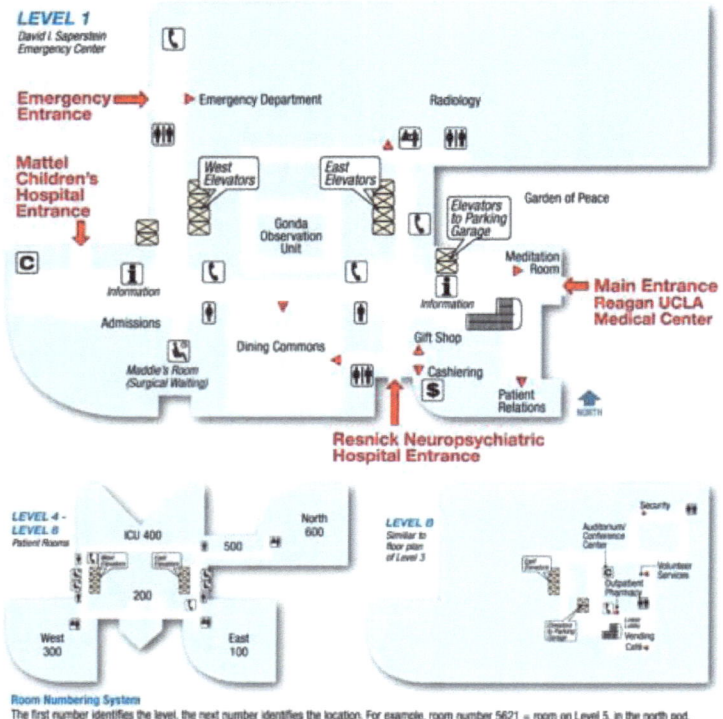

Risk

Due to the general need for hospitals, towns and cities have several large ones. The size of the hospital and its occupants are the primary concerns for survivors. Figure 25 shows how expansive hospitals are. Hospitals are potential sources for outbreaks, have numerous ill people, and contain a morgue, which can attract zombies. Another danger is the amount of potential entrances in the building. Hospitals have many entrances so there are many ways for zombies to swarm the building. With hospitals generally being at the hearts of cities or towns, a zombie swarm is a viable threat.

Figure 25: Hospital Layout[26]

Reward

Even with all the dangers that come with hospitals, the potential reward is just as great. The amount of medical supplies is extensive, and the variety of medical supplies can treat almost any injury. Food is also available for those brave enough to try and find the food court.

Raid

If possible, survivors should avoid raiding hospitals. The reward is not worth the risk since many of the medical supplies can be found in smaller pharmacies or convenience stores. For survivors that have specific medical concerns and must raid a hospital, go in a group of at least five, including someone who knows the layout of the building. Hospitals are too large to completely clear, so knowing the location of the supply room is key. When entering the hospital, clear one entrance and make sure at least two people guard it in case of a hasty retreat. The group that enters the building must do a room by room sweep on the way to the supply room if they want a safe exit in case of a zombie rush. Once the supplies have been secured, the survivors exit the way they came.

Shelter

Hospitals are not a viable long or short term shelter due to the reasons laid out in the risk section. Defending a building as large and as open as a hospital puts the group in unnecessary danger.

SUPERMARKET

Supermarkets serve the general public by offering all kinds of foods, supplies, and electronics for sale in one enormous building. They are located at many different locations in almost every town, except the most rural and isolated places.

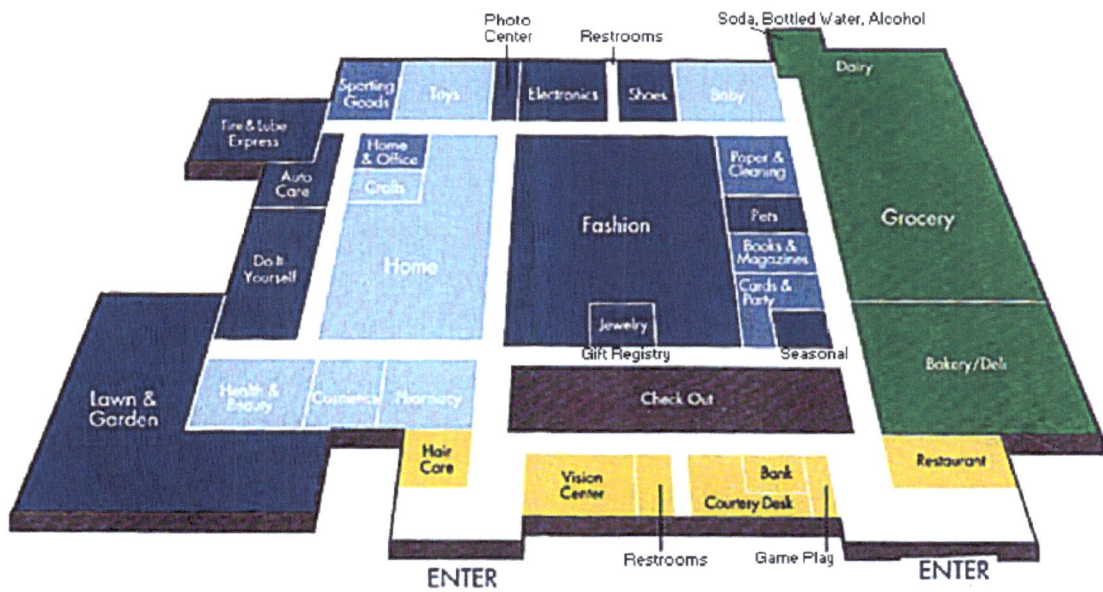

Figure 26: Supermarket Layout[27]

Risk

The most obvious danger of supermarkets is the size. Despite an open layout with aisles, there are many places for zombies to hide. Supermarkets have many different sections, as seen in Figure 26, which means plenty of places to hide and trap survivors. Since supermarkets are not always in town centers, they are safer to raid than hospitals or malls, but they still carry a high risk due to their size and their high potential to be swarmed with zombies.

Reward

The amount of goods and variety of supplies available at supermarkets makes them a one stop destination for any resupply. Supermarkets have supplies for almost every need including first aid, mechanical, food, survival, and even office supplies. The convenience and variety of these supplies comes at a cost, namely, the higher risk of entering them.

Raid

Supermarkets are best avoided if possible since there are safer places to clear that offer almost the same rewards. Convenience stores are a better alternative. If it is necessary to raid a supermarket bring at least five people. Try to find a supermarket away from town centers and leave two people to guard the entrance in case a quick escape is necessary. Three people can go into the store and clear aisle by aisle as stealthily as possible. The group should also know where they are going so they can avoid clearing out the entire supermarket.

Shelter

Supermarkets are too big to be a viable short or long term shelter. They are great for replenishing supplies but they are too attractive to zombies to spend the night in or to defend.

APARTMENT COMPLEX

Cities have apartment complexes that house many people in one building. Typical apartment complexes are multistoried buildings with apartments on each floor. These buildings are located towards the center of cities. There are some complexes that do exist outside cities but they are uncommon.

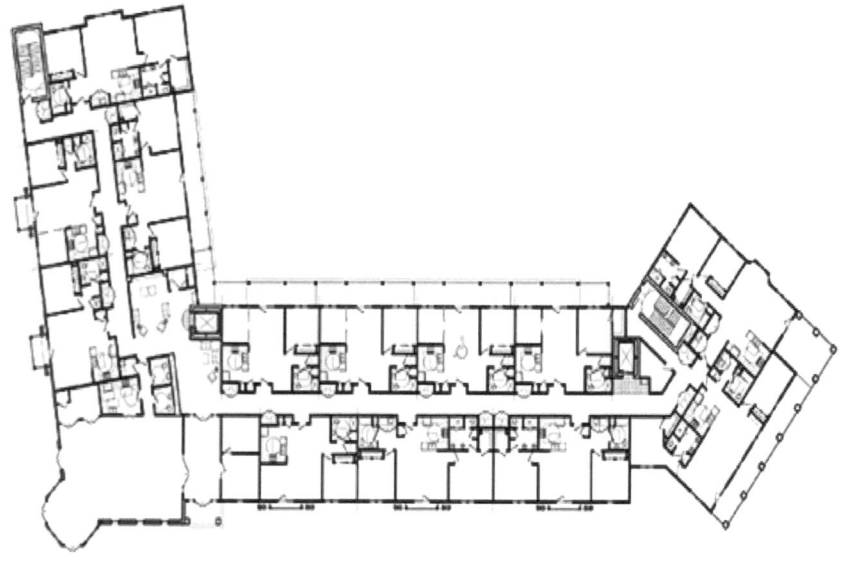

Figure 27: Apartment Complex Layout[28]

Risk

The size of apartment complexes make them hazardous since their purpose is to house many people. While they may not have as many entrances as hospitals, apartment complexes have hallways similar to hospitals, which Figure 27 displays, and which make them hard to clear out. The type of zombie in an apartment complex is also something to consider. Unlike the injured zombies present in hospitals, the zombies in apartment complexes are more likely to be active since they were probably uninjured before the outbreak. The location of the building prior to the outbreak also makes them more likely to be close to population centers, so there is always a chance for zombies to swarm the building.

Reward

Apartment complexes are hit and miss in terms of supplies. There is no guarantee of what can be found except a limited supply of food in every apartment. There are numerous apartments in a complex, so there is a chance that there will be an apartment with a fair amount of supplies. The variety of what can be found in apartments make them potential place to raid, but they are better used for short-term shelter.

Raid

Only go to apartment complexes if necessary since there are better alternatives to finding supplies and shelter, like a suburban house or convenience store. Raiding an apartment complex is similar to a hospital in the layout, but is more difficult because each room is separated. Bring at least five people and make sure that both an entrance and exit is decided on before raiding. Apartment complexes have few entrances but a fair amount of exits via fire escapes. If planning on using a fire escape, make sure the vehicle is parked by the exit and that two people can guard it. Clear the stairwell as you go to each floor so you can run back down.

Once on the floor quietly eliminate the zombies in the hallway before picking an apartment to raid. Figure 27 shows why it is important to clear hallways first. If you go straight into an apartment a zombie from the hall could follow behind you and attack. Once inside an apartment you must clear it room by room while keeping an eye on the door in case a zombie from another apartment wanders into the one being cleared. When choosing an apartment to raid, try to pick one with a fire escape.

Shelter

Apartments are easy to barricade for a night but cannot be defended in the long run due to the size and location of apartment complexes. They are best for a pit stop and time to rest.

SUBURBAN HOUSE

The suburbs are in between the city and the country. Suburban houses are generally big enough for one family and are not as enormous as a supermarket or hospital.

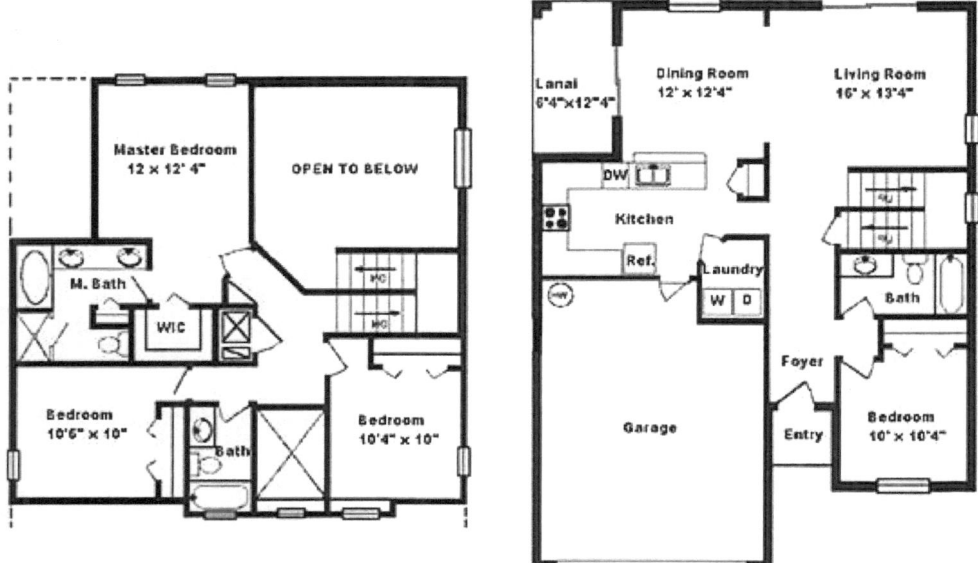

Figure 28: Suburban House Layout[29]

Risk

Houses are located outside most major population centers but can be clustered in neighborhoods. Zombie swarms are less of a threat here, but should still be a concern. Figure 28 displays one type of layout houses can have, which is different than most standard buildings so there could be many hiding places inside. There are normally only 2 or 3 entrances so it keeps potential swarms contained.

Reward

Standard supplies houses have include food, first aid, possible weapons, and other basic goods. Not all of these are guaranteed to be found but the chance is there. The main reward in raiding a house is the possibility of a shelter for a day or two but not long term.

Raid

Suburban houses are safer to clear out than big locations due to the lower potential for zombie hordes. Houses usually contain few zombies, if any, but they have nooks and hidden spots where zombies can surprise survivors who are not prepared. To clear out a house, a group must go from room to room, with at least one person keeping an eye out for zombies from neighboring rooms. Once the first floor is cleared out, move onto the second floor and so on before clearing out the basement. Clearing upwards makes it easier to escape if needed. Many suburban houses have extra rooms, such as a basement and attic. Once the house and all rooms and nooks have been purged of zombies, the house can be raided for supplies or barricaded for shelter.

Shelter

Houses are meant to be lived in, but during a zombie apocalypse they are temporary shelters depending on their location. If the suburb in which the house is located has many buildings, then it might not be viable as a shelter. If it is more isolated, then it may be a satisfactory short-term shelter, but houses are not long-term. They are difficult to defend over an extended period of time.

CONVENIENCE STORE

Small convenience stores sell food, first aid, mechanical, and other supplies in many locations ranging from downtown to the outskirts of cities and towns. They are quick stops to grab food and sometimes replenish fuel.

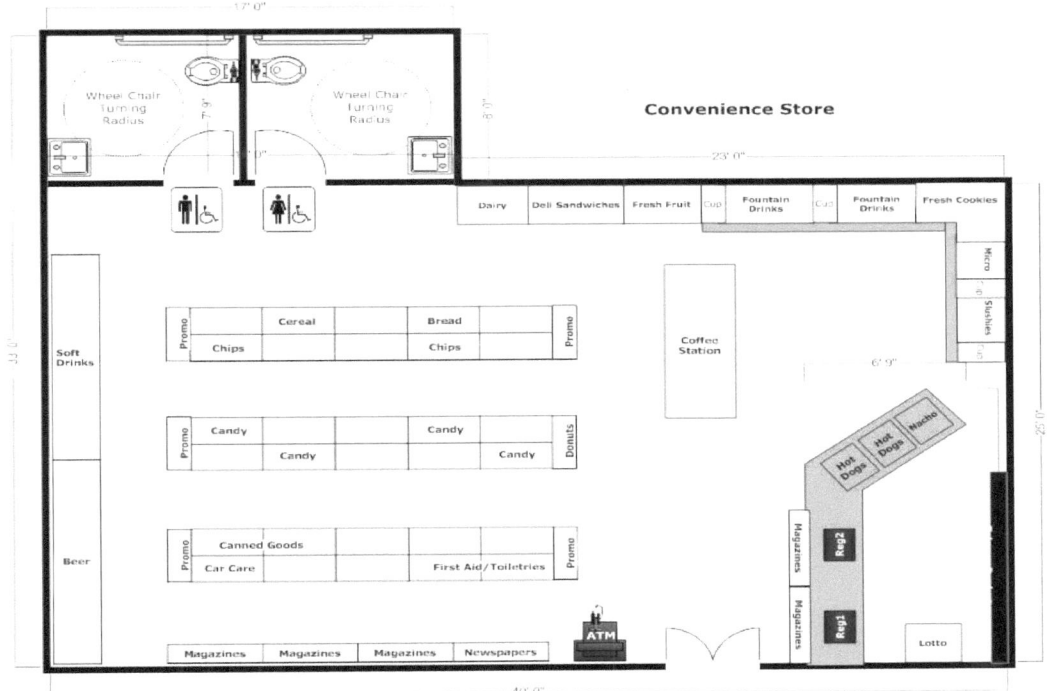

Figure 29: Convenience Store Layout[30]

Risk

Convenience stores are much smaller than supermarkets, but still contain similar supplies. Due to the great amount of convenience stores, they can be found almost anywhere including less populated areas. Figure 29 displays why convenience stores are ideal to clear out. The stores are small and wide open. There are also few entrances to convenience stores so zombie swarms are unlikely, especially in unpopulated areas. Zombies found at convenience stores are usually minimal and easy to dispatch with the aid of a group.

Reward

Despite being small, convenience stores offer a variety of supplies and food. Convenience stores have food to last a while, first aid to cover most basic injuries, and mechanical supplies to fix vehicles or other machinery. If the convenience store is in a remote enough area, it is even a viable shelter.

Raid

Doing a supply stop at a convenience store is a wise idea if the store is away from city centers. To clear a store at least four people should go. One person needs to watch the vehicle while the others go inside. Clearing the store is safer than most because of the open layout. The store should be cleared aisle by aisle, behind counters, and then bathrooms or any other remaining hidden nooks.

Shelter

Depending on the location of the convenience store, they make viable short term and possibly long term shelters. It's easy to barricade a store and to defend as long as there are few entrances. Escape from stores can also be quick if necessary. For a convenience store to be a suitable long-term shelter it must be far from the most populated of areas.

POLICE STATION

Law enforcement in every town has a police station where business is conducted, suspects can be temporarily held, and supplies are stocked. Most police stations are either downtown or on the outskirts of cities.

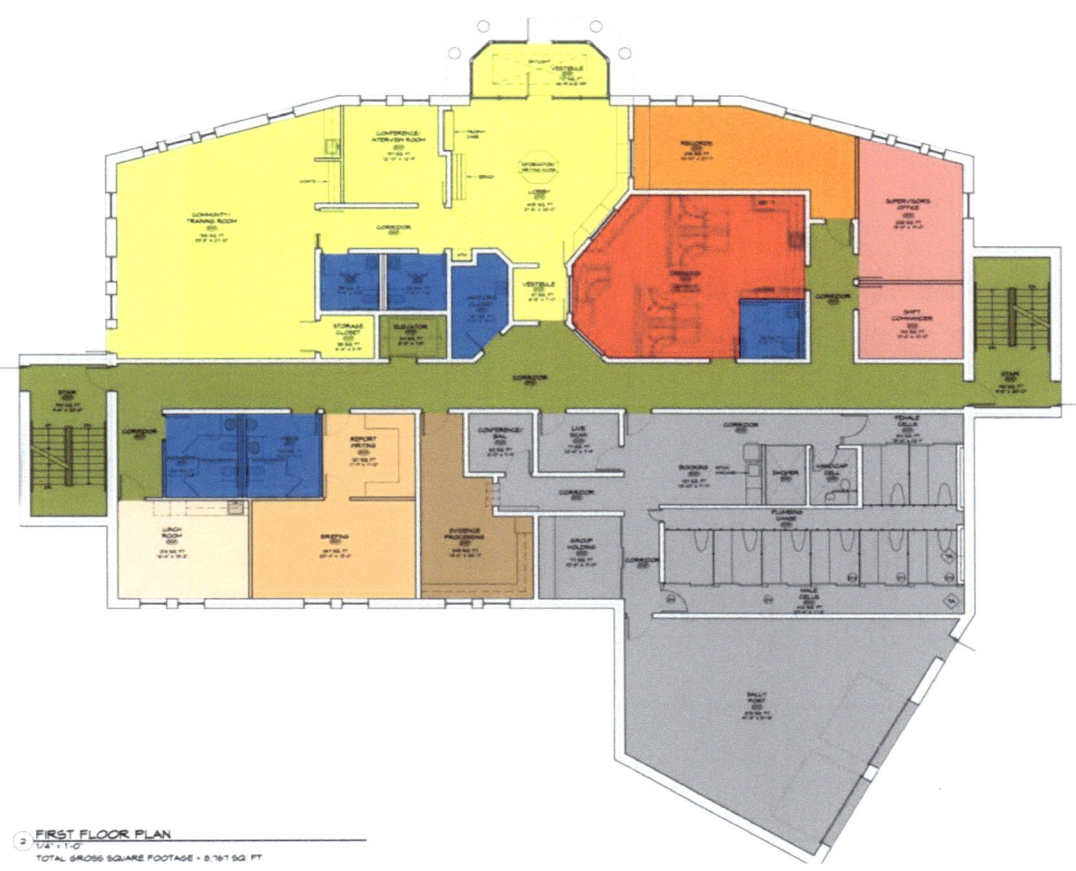

Figure 30: Police Station Layout[31]

Risk

Being close to downtown means zombies are more than likely to be around the building, but the main concern is the types of zombie that can be found in police stations. There will likely be fewer zombies in the police station than in a supermarket but more zombies than in a convenience store or house. The zombies that are found are more likely to be an intellectual or soldier type of zombie, so proceed with caution. Figure 30 shows a medium sized police station, which means plenty of rooms to clear out and places for zombies to roam. There are few entrances into a police station so if a zombie swarm happens it will be easier to manage.

Reward

Police stations are rewarding for survival supplies as well as weapons and ammunition. This unique stash makes police stations a good choice if a group is big enough and willing to risk getting the weapons needed for survival.

Raid

When raiding a police department, at least five people should be in the group. On the off chance there is an Intellectual or Soldier zombie, the group must be prepared for a tactical retreat. When clearing the police station, it must be done room by room. Silently eliminating any zombies is the best option but some may have body armor or protection. Two people must stay by the vehicle as the rest of the survivors clear out the station room by room. Avoid clearing the holding cells if possible.

Shelter

If using the police station as a shelter, make sure all rooms including the holding cells are cleared of zombies. Police stations are great for defending due to their access to protection and weapons, but being close to downtown makes it unfavorable for long-term shelter.

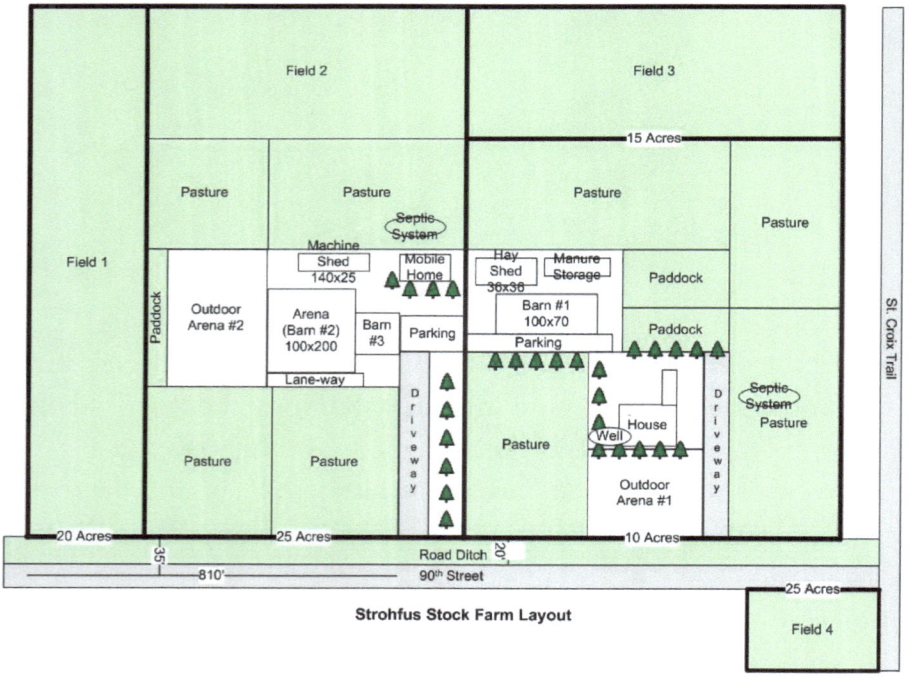

FARM

Before the zombie apocalypse farms were places where food was grown and livestock was raised. Farms are out in the country and away from cities and major towns.

Figure 31: Farm Layout[32]

Risk

Being out in the country could mean several different things for farms. It's possible the infection might not have made it to rural areas and survivors could already be at farms. Be careful of survivors that have already claimed a farm as their own; it's better to join forces instead of fighting. If the infection does make it out into the country, there will be few zombies, but they will still exist so proceed with caution and not overconfidence. Farms are wide open so it's easy to see threats, but they also contain many hidden nooks so be sure to check everything from the farmhouse to the well to the fields.

Reward

The immediate benefit of farms is not as rewarding as the long term benefit. Farms can have food stores, basic first aid supplies, machine repair equipment, and sometimes weapon caches. The true benefit of farms is the long term ability to be self-sustaining. Farms can be fortified and turned into a viable long term shelter if the right group prepares and occupies it fast enough.

Raid

Clearing out a farm can be safer than most buildings, but due to the openness of the fields and different buildings the potential for zombies hiding in places can surprise even the most prepared survivor. Clear a farm with at least four people so someone can be lookout while the other three clear the buildings one at a time. Clearing the main living area and the barns is just like clearing a house, one floor at a time and going room by room. In barns be sure to check animal pens in case zombies turned the animals into snacks. Check the fields as a group to see if any crawlers are hiding among the crops and if any zombies wandered into a well or another hidden area.

Shelter

Farms are located far enough into the country that at the start of the zombie apocalypse they are viable long term shelters. It's possible to fortify farms and grow crops or raise livestock to maintain a constant food supply for a group surviving at a farm. As time goes by, zombies may start wandering out to the country to find food in the form of animals and other survivors, so be prepared to fight off stray zombies in the future.

7

Acquiring Food

Obtaining food is essential during any catastrophe. These instructions will aid you in finding and gathering food to aid your long-term survival.

PREREQUISITES

Before following these instructions, you should read the section in this manual on the procedure of securing a location. You should have also created the Zombie Survival Kit outlined in this manual.

Warning: Obtaining food will require accessing buildings that could contain zombies or other survivors. Since survival is of upmost importance, if you suspect a zombie is inside a building, do not enter without following the procedure for securing a location. If you suspect another survivor is inside a building, establish contact with them before entering so that he or she does not assume you are a zombie and attack you.

Note: Before taking any food, know what you need. It is a good idea to grab nonperishable food and other food that will last a long time. Health is also important, so try to keep a variety of food groups using the model in Figure 32.

TYPES OF FOOD

Figure 32: The Food Pyramid[33]

Examples of food items to choose are the following:

- Canned food
- Nuts
- Peanut butter
- Energy/cereal/granola bars[34]
- Hot dogs
- Beef jerky
- Root vegetables (carrots, potatoes, etc.)[34]
- Apples
- Dried fruit
- Assorted vitamins

FINDING AND OBTAINING FOOD

1. Find a location that could potentially have food. Examples of good locations to choose are the following:

    - Supermarkets
    - Gas stations/convenience stores
    - Abandoned homes
    - Strip malls
    - Rail cars[35]
    - Food warehouses[35]

2. Enter the building. If the entrance is unlocked, enter through the main entrance. If it is locked, you can either break the door or a window or pick the lock.

3. Once you enter the building, immediately search for zombies and survivors. If there are any threats, eliminate them.

4. Barricade the entrances to ensure your safety as you scavenge.

5. Find the food you need and store it in your backpack.

6. Continue to gather supplies and food until your backpack is completely full.

7. If your location is still secure and the building is not swarmed with zombies, eat a full meal.

8. If possible, look outside the building and choose your best escape route. Your escape route could simply be the entrance, unless the entrance is swarming with zombies by the time you leave. In that case, your best escape route is the one with the least zombies.

9. Exit the building.

8

First Aid

Whether an injury occurs from battling a zombie or from the perils of everyday living, it is important to know how to treat the injury. This chapter will elaborate on two basic types of first aid: cardiopulmonary resuscitation (CPR) and administration of stitches. CPR is a procedure that is used to assist an unconscious person whose breathing or heartbeat has stopped. CPR is usually administered as a stabilization technique until paramedics or other emergency medical professionals arrive to help. However, during a zombie apocalypse, it is unlikely that such professionals will be available. This chapter will instruct the reader in delivering CPR to an adult or child. Open wounds can cause serious health issues or even death if left untreated and there may not always be professional medical assistance to treat the wound. An untreated wound can result in serious complications such as swelling, blood loss, infection, and nerve damage.[36] In some cases, death is the result of an untreated wound. It is important to clean and treat even a small wound to prevent such complications. The instructions in this chapter will detail how to clean a wound and suture it without having advanced medical care. No special training or prior medical knowledge is necessary.

HOW TO CLEAN AND SUTURE AN OPEN WOUND

An open wound is a wound that results in broken or separated skin. There are several types of open wounds: lacerations, incisions, punctures, avulsions, and abrasions. Lacerations and incisions are both cuts, but incisions are made by surgical tools. Punctures are wounds caused by a sharp object entering and then exiting the skin. Punctures are deep wounds and can appear to be a laceration if the puncturing object is large. The difference between a laceration and a puncture is shown in Figure 33. Avulsions are wounds in which skin is torn away from the body completely or on three sides leaving a skin flap. Abrasions are scratches that do not require stitches.[37]

Laceration

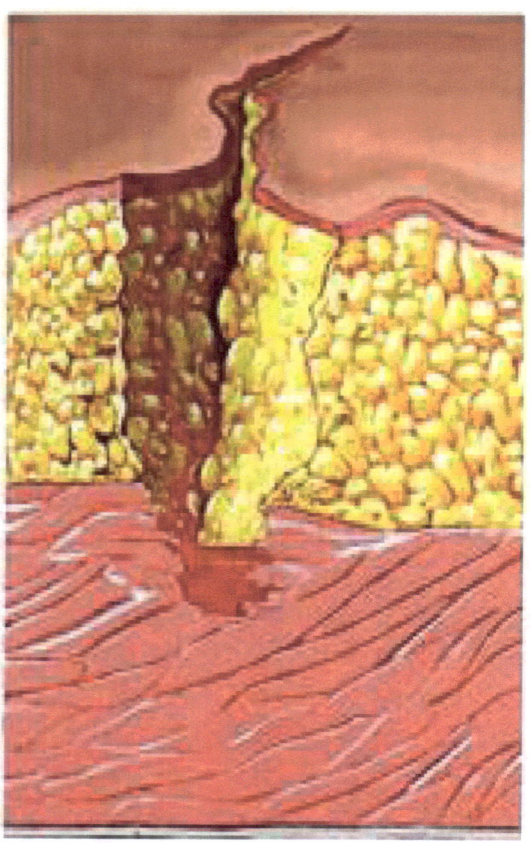

Puncture wound

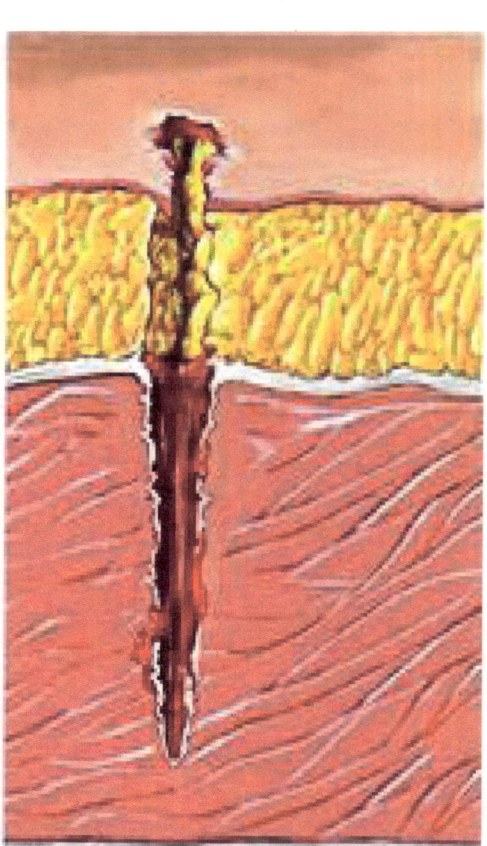

Figure 33: Laceration versus Puncture[38]

Required Materials

- Bottled water
- Sterile latex or silicon gloves (if available)
- Antiseptic (beta dine, diluted bleach, alcohol, hydrogen peroxide, iodine, or citrus)[39]
- Tweezers (if available)
- Sewing or suture needle
- Sutures or suture substitute (First Aid nylon sutures, thread, non-flavored dental floss, or fishing line)
- Sterilized gauze or breathable cloth
- Bandage
- Scissors or sharp-edged tool

 Note: If antiseptic is limited and boiling water is available, it can be used to sterilize materials. Boiling water should not be used for wound sterilization.

 Caution: After application, antiseptic must be dry before covering the wound to prevent irritation. Strong solutions of these antiseptics can cause skin burns and further infection.[39] Sterilize all materials using alcohol or boiling water to prevent infection. Sterilize the needle and cutting tools with fire, if necessary.

Prerequisites

This document assumes the following:

- The required materials are available.
- The person to receive sutures is not dying or already dead.
- The person to perform suturing knows how to boil water.

1. **Identify the type and severity of wound.** Before examining the injury, carefully remove clothing covering the area. Refer to the descriptions on page 50 to determine the type of wound: laceration, incision, puncture, avulsion, or abrasion. Once the type of wound is identified, ascertain its severity. A wound is minor if the skin of the wound will stay closed on its own and/or it is not bleeding rapidly. A wound is severe if a lot of blood has been lost and/or if the skin will not hold itself closed.

2. **Determine if the wound needs stitches.** Assess the damage of the injury. A wound needs stitches if it:

- passes through the yellow fatty layer of skin.
- bleeds continuously and rapidly.
- cannot stay closed on its own as shown in Figure 34.

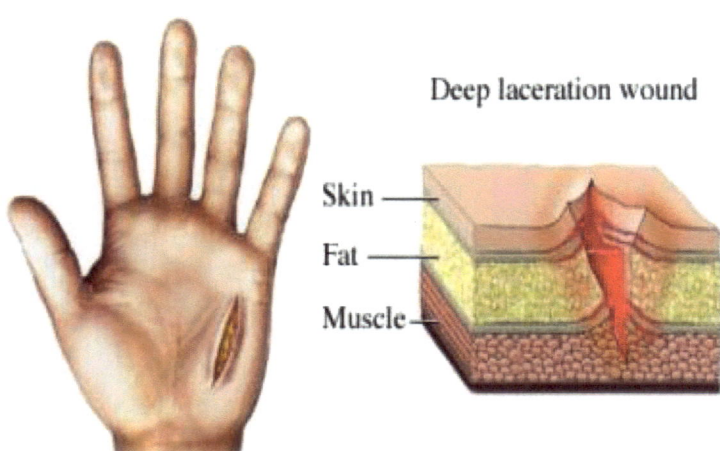

Figure 34: Deep Laceration Wound[40]

An example of a laceration that needs stitches is displayed in Figure 34. Note that the laceration cuts through the skin, fat, and muscle. The two sides of skin of the wound will not stay closed.

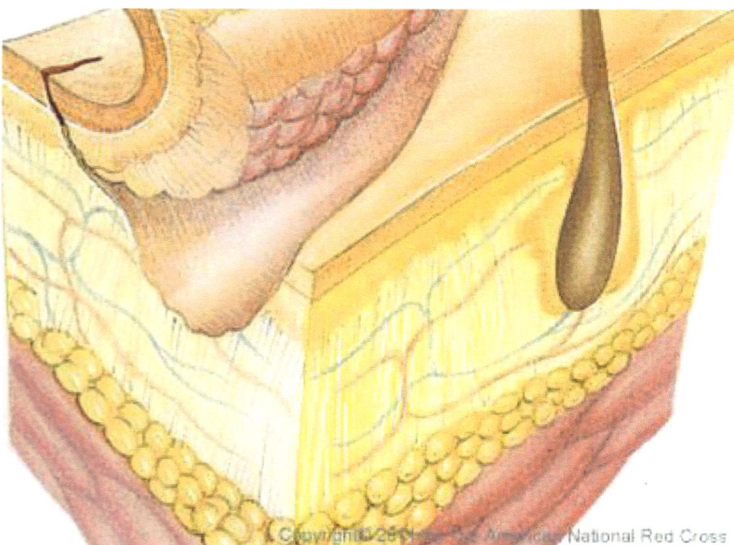

Figure 35: Skin Avulsion[41]

An example of an avulsion that requires stitches is pictured in Figure 35. Almost all avulsions that are still attached to the skin will need stitches. Avulsions where the skin is completely removed from the body cannot be sutured. Avulsions can be detached from the rest of the body on two or three sides.

3. **Sterilize all materials.** Before cleaning the wound, sterilize any materials that will come in contact with it. Sterilize gloves (if available) by spraying them with an antiseptic or submerging them in an antiseptic solution. If gloves are unavailable, sterilize hands in the same way. Use the antiseptic or boiling water to sterilize the tweezers (if available), needle, sutures or suture substitutes, gauze or breathable cloth, bandaging materials, and scissors or sharp-edged tool.

 Note: Do not use boiling water to sterilize gauze, cloth, or bandages. The materials will become saturated with water and be unusable.

4. **Clean the wound.** After the materials have been sterilized, clean the wound. This will be painful, but will prevent infection or other complications. First use the bottled water to wash away as much blood as possible, especially clotted blood. Then pour the water into the wound by holding the wound open with sterilized fingers or hands. Use a sterile cloth or rag to wash any dirt or other substance away from the wound.

5. **Remove debris from the wound.** While holding the wound open, use tweezers or fingers to remove and dirt, gravel, or other foreign objects from the wound. Occasionally wash bottled water over the cut if the blood impairs the ability to see debris. After clearing all objects out of the wound, apply antiseptic. Dilute the antiseptic with bottled water if it is highly concentrated.

6. **Prepare needle and suture material.** Thread the sterile suture or suture substitute through the eye of the needle as shown in Figure 36. The needle may either be a simple sewing needle or a medical suture needle. A suture needle will be curved. After inserting the suture material through the eye of the needle, tie in a knot.

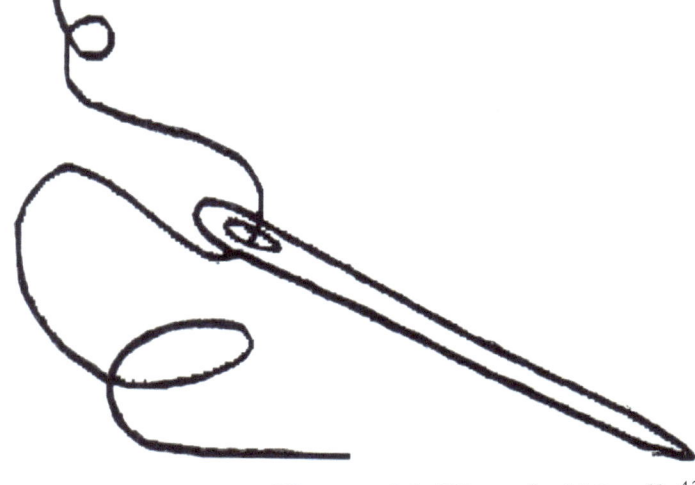

Figure 36: Threaded Needle[42]

7. **Pull wound together and make first interrupted suture.** Insert the threaded needle into the skin near the center of the wound and approximately half a centimeter away from the edge of the wound. Pull the needle through and reinsert the needle underneath the skin on the other side of the wound. Use the scissors or cutting tool to detach the suture material from the needle and to cut the suture material on the original side of the wound. Leave about an inch of suture material on each side of the wound. Then tie the two ends in a double knot. Refer to Figure 37 for help.

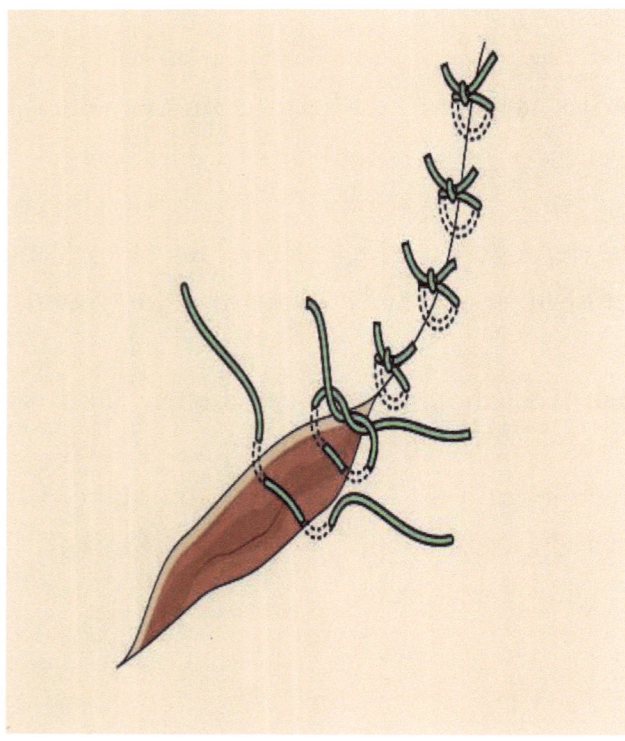

8. **Continue with sutures.** Make the next suture with the same steps described in step 7, working outward from the center in both directions until the sutures reach the edge of the wound on both sides.

9. **Bandage stitched wound.** Using gauze or breathable cloth, loosely cover the sutured wound. To hold the covering in place, use a bandage (if available) or tie another piece of cloth or gauze around the covering. Keep the wound covered for 24-48 hours and then remove the bandaging.

Figure 37: Wound Sutures[43]

Caution: Avoid getting the sutures in water or dirt to prevent infection.

HOW TO ADMINISTER CARDIOPULMONARY RESUSCITATION (CPR)

Cardiopulmonary resuscitation is a procedure that restarts blood flow and breathing and that can be performed without any medical equipment. Before beginning CPR, determine whether the individual experiencing an emergency is in need of CPR. An individual needs CPR if he or she:

- is unconscious.
- has stopped breathing.
- has no pulse or heartbeat.

Prerequisites

The instructions for performing CPR assume the following:

- the individual upon which CPR will be administered has not been medically dead (no pulse or breathing) for longer than ten minutes.[44]
- the individual is not a zombie at the time CPR will be performed.
- the reader knows how to check for a pulse.

1. **Identify whether the individual is a zombie.** Refer to Chapter 3: Types of Zombies or Chapter 5: Forming a Safety Group. If the individual is a zombie and they have not noticed you, quickly and quietly flee or hide. Only attempt to eliminate the zombie if highly trained and carrying an effective elimination weapon (refer to Chapter 4: Weapons). If the individual is not a zombie, continue to step 2.

 Caution! Use extreme caution administering CPR. If the person has recently been infected with a zombie parasite or virus, he or she may not show symptoms immediately.

2. **Determine if the individual meets the requirements and prerequisites listed above.** To identify if the individual is unconscious, shake his or her shoulder gently and ask loudly if he or she is okay. If there is no response, continue to step 3. If there is a response, check the individual's pulse and breathing to determine his or her condition.

3. **If an automatic external defibrillator (AED) is available, deliver one shock as instructed by the device.** After delivering one shock, continue to step 4. If an AED is unavailable, continue to step 4.[44]

4. **Place the individual on his or her back.** They should be resting on a stable surface.

5. **Place the heel of one hand on the center of the person's chest.** Put the other hand on top of the first hand. Make sure shoulders are positioned above hands and keep elbows straight. The proper position is shown in Figure 38.

6. **Use the upper body and not only arms to push down firmly on the individual's chest at least 2 inches.** This is called a chest compression. Repeat the compression approximately 100 times per minute.

7. **After completing 30 chest compressions, continue to step 8.** The next steps will instruct how to clear the airway and give rescue breaths.

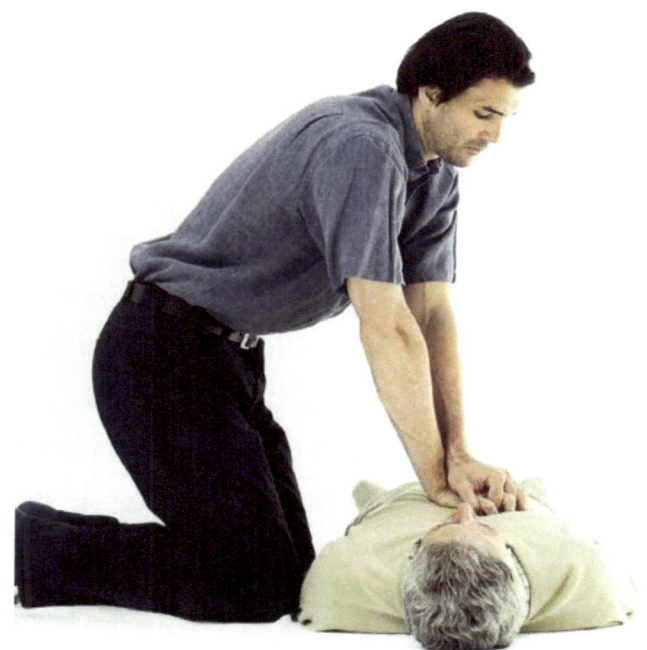

Figure 38: Chest Compression[45]

Warning: Do not go on to step 8 if the cause of unconsciousness or injury is unknown. If the individual sustained the injury by engaging a zombie, they may be infected. Only proceed to step 8 if the individual is 100 percent human and the injury was sustained without contact to a zombie.

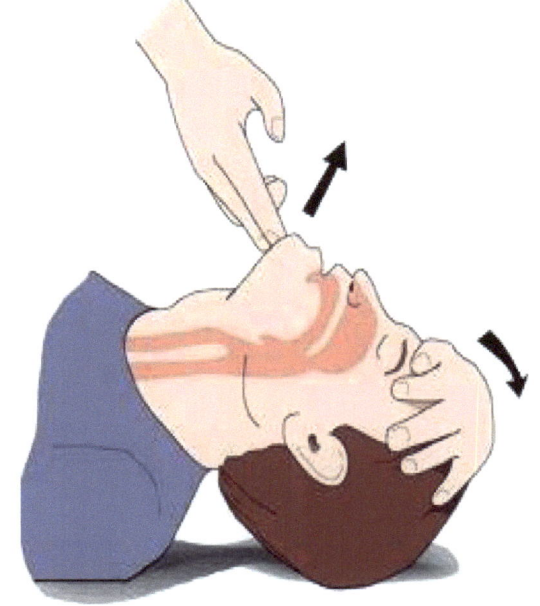

8. **Open the individual's airway using the head-tilt, chin-lift maneuver.** Slowly tilt the head back by placing a hand on the person's forehead. At the same time, gently move the chin up and forwards. This will open the airway as shown in Figure 39.

9. **Check for signs of normal breathing.** Listen for normal breath sounds, look for movement in the chest, and feel for the individual's breath on cheek or ear. If the individual is not breathing normally, continue to step 10.

Figure 39: Clearing the Airway[46]

10. **Pinch the nostrils shut firmly with one hand.** Making sure the airway is open as described in step 8, cover the individual's mouth with yours and make a seal. Breathe into the mouth and look to see if the chest rises. If it does rise, breathe a second breath into the mouth. If not, repeat step 8 and give the second breath.

11. **After giving two rescue breaths, resume chest compressions as described in steps 5 and 6.** Complete 30 more chest compressions and again give two rescue breaths. 30 compressions and two breaths is one cycle. After 5 cycles or about 2 minutes, check for movement in the individual. If there is movement, discontinue compressions and rescue breathing. If there is not movement and an AED is available, deliver one shock and then continue with chest compressions for two more minutes. Then deliver a second shock. If an AED is unavailable, continue to step 12.

12. **Continue CPR until the individual shows signs of movement.** After 10-12 minutes with no movement, pulse, or breathing, compressions and breaths may be stopped.

Frequently Asked Questions

WHAT IS A ZOMBIE?

A zombie is a creature that craves human flesh. A zombie can be a reanimated corpse or a human that has been compromised by a parasite or virus that causes zombie-like behavior. Zombie behavior can include loss of motor control, single-minded direction, primal instincts, and desire to infect humans.

HOW OFTEN DO ZOMBIES FEED?

Depending on the type of zombie, how often the zombie feeds would differ. A virus would most likely cause the zombie to feed as often as a regular person, while a parasite could cause the zombie to feed indefinitely.

DO ZOMBIES LIVE FOREVER?

No—after many years, the zombie's body will decay to the point where it can no longer function.[47]

WHEN WILL A ZOMBIE APOCALYPSE LIKELY OCCUR?

No one knows when a zombie apocalypse will occur. It could be tomorrow or in 100 years. The important thing is to be prepared, because being prepared for a zombie apocalypse will prepare you for other disasters as well.

DURING THE APOCALYPSE, WILL SOCIETY COLLAPSE?

A zombie apocalypse would require an extremely aggressive military response in order to keep society from collapsing. In a populated city, this would mean a response time of 3-8 days. After 8 days with no aggressive response, society could collapse.[48]

WHAT SHOULD I DO WHEN I FIRST HEAR OF AN OUTBREAK BUT BEFORE SOCIETY HAS COLLAPSED?

First, you should make sure you are prepared and have the Zombie Survival Kit (especially the radio!) and a reliable vehicle. Then, gather a group and head to an unpopulated area. This will reduce the risk of infection.

WHERE CAN I FIND THE SUPPLIES FOR THE ZOMBIE SURVIVAL KIT AND THE FIRST AID KIT?

All of the supplies for the Zombie Survival Kit, including the First Aid kit, can be ordered online at www.amazon.com and most of them can also be found at sporting goods stores. The First Aid kit can also be purchased from the American Red Cross at www.RedCross.org.

WHAT IS A GOOD VEHICLE TO HAVE FOR THE ZOMBIE APOCALYPSE?

While any vehicle is a good vehicle to have during the zombie apocalypse, the best vehicle would be a fuel-efficient car with a bicycle. The car could get you to an unpopulated area and carry many supplies, and you will be able to use the bicycle for transportation once you run out of gas.

WHAT IS A GOOD LOCATION TO BE IN DURING THE ZOMBIE APOCALYPSE?

A farm in an extremely unpopulated area would be the best location in a zombie apocalypse. This would reduce the risk of infection and offer a potential food source. A rural farm provides a clear view for miles so threats such as zombies or scavengers can be quickly spotted and apprehended. Survivors can begin farming and growing their own crops as well as raising livestock for food or trade purposes.

REFERENCES

1. Zombiepedia. Melee weapons [Internet]. [cited Mar 23 2013]. Available from: http://zombie.wikia.com/wiki/Melee_weapons

2. Cracked. Zombie survival [Internet]. [cited Mar 23 2013]. Available from: http://www.cracked.com /funny-1077-zombie-survival/

3. Lauren Davis. 10 tips for surviving the zombie apocalypse [Internet]. [cited Mar 23 2013]. Available from: http://io9.com/5148637/10-tips-for-surviving-the-zombie-apocalypse

4. 2012 Zombie Survival Kit. Zombie survival pack for individuals [Internet]. [cited Feb 18 2013]. Available from: http://zombiesurvivalkit.org/

5. First Baptist Church. Food pantry [Internet]. [cited Feb 18 2013]. Available from: http://www.fbcmedford.com/foodpantry.htm

6. Woman's Day. Eight emergency kit essentials [Internet]. [cited Feb 18 2013]. Available from: http://www.womansday.com/life/battery-operated-radio#slide-6

7. The Shofar. The history of zombies [Internet]. 2012 [cited Mar 14 2013]. Available from: http://shofarmdchs.wordpress.com/2012/11/27/the-history-of-zombies/

8. Mandal A. News Medical. What is a virus? [Internet]. [cited Mar 14 2013]. Available from: http://www.news-medical.net/health/What-is-a-Virus.aspx

9. Civil Service of Pakistan: Cell Biology and terms. Micro-organisms causing disease [Internet]. [cited Mar 14 2013]. Available from: http://upload.wikimedia.org/wikipedia/commons/b/b6/Influenza_geneticshift.jpg

10. Than K. National Geographic. "Zombie virus" possible via rabies-flu hybrid? [Internet]. 2010 [cited Mar 14 2013]. Available from: http://news.nationalgeographic.com/news/2010/10/1001027-rabies-influenza-zombie-virus-science/

11. Centers for Disease Control and Prevention. Parasites [Internet]. 2010 [cited Mar 14 2013]. Available from: http://www.cdc.gov/parasites/about.html

12. News Medical. What is neuromodulation? [Internet]. [cited Mar 14 2013]. Available from: http://www.news-medical.net/health/What-is-Neuromodulation.aspx

13. Knight K. The Journal of Experimental Biology. How pernicious parasites turn victims into zombies [Internet]. 2013 [cited Mar 15 2013]. Available from: http://jeb.biologists.org/content/216/1/i.full

14. Dvorsky G. Institute for Ethics and Emerging Technologies. How to engineer a zombie virus [Internet]. 2010 [cited Mar 15 2013]. Available from: http://ieet.org/index.php/IEET/more/dvorsky20101219

15. Centers for Disease Control and Prevention. Dicrocoeliasis [Internet]. 2009 [cited Mar 15 2013]. Available from: http://www.dpd.cdc.gov/dpdx/images/ParasiteImages/A-F/Dicrocoeliasis/Dicrocoelium_LifeCycle.gif

16. BCJ Media. Crawling Zombie [Internet]. 2012 [cited Feb 12 2013]. Available from: http://bcjmedia.com/wp/wp-content/uploads/2012/04/20120226_bcj_3388.jpg

17. Greg Nicotero. American movie classics [Internet]. TWD Productions LLC; 2011 [cited Feb 12 2013]. Available from: http://comicbooked.comicbookedllc.netdna-cdn.com/wp-content/uploads/2011/10/the-walking-dead-season-2-zombie-still-2.jpg

18. FX stunt school [Internet]. 2013 [cited Feb 13 2013]. Available from: http://www.plugdinmagazine.com/resources/zombiefire.jpg

19. Fast Zombies [Internet]. [cited Feb 13 2013]. Available from: http://3.bp.blogspot.com/-lbWHTqK7_88/UJ7HZjhs2aI/AAAAAAAADCk/3SK7CjiSVsU/s1600/FastZombies.jpg

20. Zombies. 7chan. *7chan* [Internet]. 2013 [cited Feb 13 2013]. Available from: https://7chan.org/zom/src/133228238030.jpg

21. Zombie Pumpkins. Closing in on 100 days [Internet]. 2009 [cited Feb 13 2013]. Available from: http://i682.photobucket.com/albums/vv190/louie123-321/18.jpg

22. Merriam-Webster. Definition of gun [Internet]. [cited Feb 9 2013]. Available from: http://www.merriam-webster.com/dictionary/gun

23. Info 4 Guns. Fiream parts [Internet]. [cited Feb 9 2013]. Available from http://www.info4guns.com/firearms_parts.html

24. Overstock. Defender black 9-inch spring-assisted folding pocket knife [Internet]. [cited Feb 9 2013]. Available from: http://www.overstock.com/Sports-Toys/Defender-Black-9-inch-Spring-assisted-Folding-Pocket-Knife/6700340/product.html

25. Human Events. 'Zombie Invasion' training planned for troops on Halloween [Internet]. [cited Feb 21 2013]. Available from: http://www.humanevents.com/2012/10/29/zombie-invasion-training-planned-for-troops-on-halloween/

26. Semel Institute. Ronald Reagan UCLA Medical Center [Internet]. [cited March 19 2013].Available from http://www.semel.ucla.edu/maps/resnick

27. My Coldwater. Local store maps- Walmart [Internet]. [cited March 25 2013]. Available from http://www.mycoldwater.com/walmart_map.html

28. Moyer House. Apartment building map [Internet]. [cited March 25 2013]. Available from http://www.moyerhouse.org/page/7636-apartment-building-map

29. Sun-Orlando. Floor plan [Internet]. [cited March 19 2013] Available from http://www.sun-orlando.com/photos/floor_plan.html

30. SmartDraw. Convenience Store Layout Example. [cited March 25 2013]. Available from: http://www.smartdraw.com/examples/view/convenience+store+layout/

31. Webster Police Department. New police station project: first floor layout proposal [Internet]. [cited March 19 2013]. Available from http://www.websterpolice.com/newstation.shtml

32. Strohfus Stock Farm. Facilities [Internet]. [cited April 1 2013]. Available from http://www.strohfusstockfarm.com/Documents/Facilities.aspx

33. United States Department of Agriculture. My pyramid tracker [Internet]. [cited Feb 27 2013]. Available from: http://www.fns.usda.gov/eatsmartplayhardhealthy lifestyle/tools/mypyramidtracker.htm

34. PBS Food. 13 foods you need to survive the zombie apocalypse [Internet]. [cited Feb 25 2013]. Available from: http://www.pbs.org/food/features/13-foods-you-need-to-survive-a-zombie-apocalypse/

35. The Wolf. Where to find food and supplies in the post apocalypse [Internet]. [cited Feb 25 2013]. Available from: http://daily-survival.blogspot.com/2010/04/where-to-find-food-and-supplies-in-post.html

36. Saint Agnes Hospital. Saint Agnes Hospital. Assisting you in wound care [Internet]. 2012 [cited Feb 22 2013]. Available from: http://www.stagnes.org/index.php/our-specialties/wound-center/

37. Brouhard R. About.com First Aid. About.com Guide. Do I Need Stitches? [Internet]. 2013 [cited Feb 22 2013]. Available from: http://firstaid.about.com/od/softtissueinjuries/a/06_stitches.htm.

38. Singapore sports and orthopaedics clinic. Lacerations Wound. Treatment & Types [Internet]. [cited Feb 22 2013]. Available from: http://www.orthopaedics.com.sg/treatments/laceration-wound.

39. Internet FAQs archive. Internet FAQs archive. Antiseptics, Information about antiseptics [Internet]. [cited Feb 23 2013]. Available from: http://www.faqs.org/health/topics/76/Antiseptics.html.

40. University of Virginia Health System. Laceration Repair. Laceration Repair--UVA Health [Internet]. [cited Feb 23 2013]. Available from: http://uvahealth.com/services/plastic-surgery/conditions-treatments/101013.

41. Sharecare. American Red Cross, What Is an Avulsion? [Internet]. [cited Feb 26 2013]. Available from: http://www.sharecare.com/question/what-is-an-avulsion.

42. Satsang: June 2010 [Internet]. [cited Feb 26 2013]. Available from: http://sundaysatsang.blogspot.com/2010_06_01_archive.html.

43. ShortWhiteCoats. How to Suture a Wound: A Video Tutorial [Internet]. [cited Feb 24 2013]. Available from: http://shortwhitecoats.com/2011/how-to-suture-a-wound-a-video-tutorial.

44. Mayo Clinic. Cardiopulmonary resuscitation (CPR): first aid [Internet]. 2012 [cited Mar 24 2013]. Available from: http://www.mayoclinic.com/health/first-aid-cpr/FA00061.

45. Vector Health & Safety. CPR courses [Internet]. [cited Mar 24 2013]. Available from: http://www.vector-health.com/product-1.htm.

46. The Walking Pages. First aid. Airway [Internet]. 2012 [cited Mar 24 2014]. Available from: http://www.henleyandbrown.plus.com/walking/info/first_aid.html

47. Zombie Crisis. Frequently asked questions. 2010. Available from: http://www.zombiecrisis.org/survival_faqs.php

48. Brown, Nathan Robert. 2010. The complete idiot's guide to zombies. New York, NY: Penguin

INDEX